Debra Shipley and Mary Peplow are freelance journalists working in both broadcasting and the national press. Their interests are wide and varied, ranging from parks to pageantry, culture to crafts.

By the same authors

London for Free
London Fun Book

DEBRA SHIPLEY
AND MARY PEPLOW

Edinburgh for Free

GRAFTON BOOKS

A Division of the Collins Publishing Group

LONDON GLASGOW
TORONTO SYDNEY AUCKLAND

Grafton Books
A Division of the Collins Publishing Group
8 Grafton Street, London W1X 3LA

Published by Grafton Books 1986

ISBN 0-586-06580-6

Printed and bound in Great Britain by
Collins, Glasgow

Set in Times

Contents

Acknowledgements

First, we'd like to say a big thank you to Ian Paten, our editor, for his patience throughout the project and to Richard Atkinson for his invaluable support and encouragement. We're also tremendously grateful to the Edinburgh Tourist Board and the Scottish Tourist Board for providing us with stacks of information to guide us through our research, and to British Rail and British Caledonian Airways for proving that Edinburgh, the 'Athens of the North', is easily accessible by train and air from all parts of the country.

THE RT. HON.

JOHN McKAY

Edinburgh For Free is such an imaginative idea for a book. We all love the City and I am deeply grateful that the two authors should have considered Edinburgh. The thorough and painstaking research that has been undertaken will I know be of enormous benefit and interest not only to the thousands of visitors who come to see us but to a great many residents also.

I do hope that those who read this book will set out to explore the beautiful City of Edinburgh and see just how much can be done for free!

Lord Provost

Preface

One of the first people we told about this guidebook to all that is free in Edinburgh was a Scotsman. 'That'll go down well in Scotland,' he said with a wry grin, seeing the funny side immediately. The Scots have, of course, become the butt of countless jokes about keeping a tight hold on their purse-strings. But one thing's for certain – there's nothing mean about their capital city. Edinburgh is generous and welcoming to the extreme, with something to offer everyone whatever their age or interests.

Sir Walter Scott described Edinburgh as 'Mine own romantic town', Robert Louis Stevenson referred to it affectionately as 'this profusion of eccentricities, this dream of masonry and living rock', and we found it all this and much more. We quickly realized that it's a city full of character and unique appeal – a truly individual place. Like most people, we'd heard of the Royal Mile and the New Town long before we began our research, but it was only when we walked the cobbled lanes and wide esplanades and explored the parklands that we discovered the towering tenements, wind-swept open spaces, hidden courtyards and quirky museums.

It was only then that we could begin to build up our own very personal picture of this historic city, and we hope *Edinburgh for Free* will help you do the same. There's a very special atmosphere in 'Auld Reekie' which we're sure you'll experience and fall in love with. We know you'll want to visit it time and again.

If you are lucky enough to live in Edinburgh or if you

are a visitor with lots of time to spare then we'd rec-
ommend seeing everything that's free in Edinburgh – we
have, and enjoyed every minute! But if your time is
limited then there are some attractions we feel you really
shouldn't miss and these are marked throughout with an
asterisk. At the back of the book there are four walks
which take you through Edinburgh past and present.
These walks, which you can easily fit into a weekend
stay, will give you a true taste of Scotland's capital city.
And it really is best to discover Edinburgh on foot (and
it's free!)

Most of the places in the book are within walking
distance of the city centre. To help you find your way
around pick up a free map from the Tourist Information
Centre at Waverley Market, Princes Street (Tel: 031-557
2727) or simply ask a passer-by – he or she will probably
take you there personally! To reach the further-flung
places there's a network of buses which is both convenient
and efficient. We've indicated some of the main bus
routes but you can get a free bus route planner from the
Tourist Information Centre at Waverley Market, Princes
Street (tel: 031-557 2727).

There's so much to see and do in Edinburgh that's
free, we couldn't hope to include everything, so if you've
discovered something you feel deserves a mention then
please let us know. Also, although the times, addresses
and telephone numbers were correct at the time of going
to press, we'd like to hear from you if you find anything
that has changed.

We hope that, like us, you'll spend many a happy day
in this beautiful city and enjoy the very best of everything
that makes up *Edinburgh for Free*.

CHAPTER ONE
Parks and Open Spaces

*ARTHUR'S SEAT, Holyrood Park

Arthur's Seat, an extinct volcano of red igneous rock, provides superb views over the city to the Pentland Hills (*see page 25*) in one direction and to the Firth of Forth in the other. Towering some 820 feet (250m) out of Holyrood Park (*see page 21*), this is the perfect spot to sit and look down on Holyroodhouse Palace and let your imagination drift. On a winter's evening Holyrood shimmers romantically and it's easy to imagine its mistress Mary Queen of Scots who, it is said, 'danced, cried, laughed, saw murder done, married and met failure here.'

Open: all the time

EXTRA . . . EXTRA . . . A number of claims are made for the origin of the name Arthur's Seat. It may relate to the 6th-century Prince Arthur of Strathclyde; or it might be a corruption of *Ard Thor*, which is Gaelic for 'Height of Thor'.

BLACKFORD HILL

This park which adjoins the Hermitage of Braid (*see page 20*) is the ideal place for a good long country ramble, especially if you go armed with a pair of binoculars. Blackford Pond, a natural pond, has become a popular nesting place for mallards and other waterfowl and you can spend many a happy hour watching the activity around the water. Towards the top of the hill stands the Royal Observatory with its green copper rounded domes. Built in 1896, this is now a research establishment and houses much advanced astronomical equipment.

Unfortunately, you have to pay to go inside the Royal Observatory, but if you climb to the top of the 539 foot (165m) summit, you'll be rewarded with some spectacular views over the city and surrounding countryside. To the south lie the Braid Hills (*see below*), now a golf course and the Hermitage of Braid (*see page 20*), and to the north, Calton Hill (*see page 17*) and Arthur's Seat (*see page 13*). Blackford Quarry is at the foot of the hill, and the Agassiz stone is exhibited at the entrance. This is named after the Swiss naturalist Louis Agassiz (1807–73) who believed he had found the marks of glaciers from the last Ice Age.

Bus: 5, 11, 15, 16
Open: all the time

EXTRA . . . EXTRA . . . Lord Cockburn, distinguished judge and man of letters of the late 18th century, often used to walk through the park. He wrote, 'There was a pond [Blackford Pond] where I learned to skate – the most delightful of all exercises, and one which I have practised with unfailing ardour ever since.' The pond still freezes over in the winter months.

BRAID HILLS

Now the home of the two Braid Hills golf courses, it's best to walk the hills on a Sunday when there's no golf being played and you can cross the course. Choose a clear day so that you can enjoy the views from the top – you're 600 feet (182m) above sea level and the whole of Edinburgh seems to open up to you. One of the most spectacular views is of the estuary of the Forth with its gleaming water and tiny islands. Look further and you may be able to identify the peak of Ben Lomond. You'll need a good pair of walking shoes as the going gets pretty rough at times.

Bus: 11, 15, 16
Open: all the time

EXTRA . . . EXTRA . . . Until the 19th century the area stretching south from The Meadows (*see page 24*) to the Braid Hills was known as the Great Forest of Drumselch, home of many 'hartis, hindis, toddis [foxes] and siclike manner of beasties'.

BRUNTSFIELD LINKS, off Melville Drive

Heavily planted with trees, this park just a mile south of Edinburgh Castle (*see page 42*) and adjacent to The Meadows (*see page 24*) was once a famous golf course. Indeed, the date of the Golf Tavern which overlooks the links is 1456, so golf has obviously been played here since the 15th century. The original course is no longer there – but the past still lingers on in the shape of a pitch and putt course and putting green. It's a pleasant place for a short stroll or picnic.

Open: all the time

EXTRA . . . EXTRA . . . The Bruntsfield Links Golfing Society, founded in 1761, is thought to be the third or fourth oldest golf club in the world.

CALTON BURYING GROUNDS, Waterloo Place

If you've always thought graveyards were boring places to be avoided, think again. Calton Burying Grounds are dominated by a sad reminder of legal iniquity – a huge obelisk known as Martyr's Memorial, dedicated to five early Chartists. They were members of a universal suffrage movement who, in 1793, were tried for treason, found guilty and sentenced to transportation. Their crime? They had advocated parliamentary reform. On the west side of the burying grounds is a statue of Abraham Lincoln – the first statue of an American president to be erected in Britain. Look out too for a circular Roman-style tomb designed in 1777 by Robert Adam as a memorial to the philosopher and historian David Hume (1711–76). But it's the view which makes the short walk up from Princes Street worth the effort: Arthur's Seat (*see page 13*), Waverley Bridge, the Old Town (*see Walk 3   The Royal Mile, page 147*), Edinburgh Castle (*see page 42*) and the clock tower of the North British Hotel span out in a fascinating panorama.

Open: daily˙

EXTRA . . . EXTRA . . . Nearby Calton Road and Waterloo Place form what was the first road-over-road system in Scotland.

---

*CALTON HILL, off Regent Road

You must, must, climb this hill in the city centre, it's 350 feet (107m) above sea level and the views are fantastic. Choose a clear day, preferably with a light breeze, and enjoy the walk. Take the winding path to the summit (don't take the steps to the right, keep to the wide path) and you'll be rewarded with a spectacular view of the Firth of Forth over rows of Georgian roof-tops. Next in sight as you circle the hill is the grand sweep of Arthur's Seat (*see page 13*) and the pretty turrets of the Palace of Holyroodhouse (*see Holyrood Park, page 21*). Further round still is the cluster of Edinburgh's Old Town (*see Walk 3 The Royal Mile, page 147*) and the castle (*see page 42*) which seems surprisingly far away. The winding route up Calton Hill will also take you past Nelson Monument (*see page 52*), City Memorial, National Monument (*see page 51*) and Dugald Stewart Memorial (*see page 42*).

Open: all the time

EXTRA . . . EXTRA . . . Calton Hill probably gets its name from the Gaelic, *Choille Dun* (a hill covered with bushes).

CORSTORPHINE HILL

A visit to this woody hill is usually combined with a trip to the zoo (entrance fee) but at 531 feet (162m) it's worth visiting just for the excellent panoramic view it provides of the city. Beyond the 'shaved' contours of the golf course spreads Edinburgh and, in the distance, the blue waters of the Firth. On a clear day you can see the

National Monument on Calton Hill (*see page 17*), Edinburgh Castle (*see page 42*) and Arthur's Seat (*see page 13*).

Bus: 12, 26, 31
Open: all the time

EXTRA . . . EXTRA . . . On Corstorphine Hill is Clermiston Tower, built to celebrate the centenary of the birth of Sir Walter Scott.

DEAN BANK TO STOCKBRIDGE, Water of Leith Walkway

This is a beautiful walk at any time of year, but during the autumn it becomes spectacular. At the start of the walk ash, elm, sycamore and lime trees provide a lush canopy. Dropped leaves float peacefully on the Water while overhanging branches play with their own reflections. Robin, greenfinch, blackbird and willow warbler are all common and if you're lucky you may just catch a glimpse of a kingfisher. Emerging from this wooded section of the walk you enter Dean Village (*see page 127*) which seems timeless, if a little too clean. From here you can pick up the waterside pathway which will take you all the way to Stockbridge (*see page 134*).

Bus: 18, 20, 41
Open: all the time

EXTRA . . . EXTRA . . . Your walk will take you past St Bernard's Mineral Well – a temple in an idyllic setting.

FORTH ROAD BRIDGE

You can't find a much more open space than the top of the Forth Road Bridge! Although car drivers pay a toll to cross, pedestrians are free to walk and it really is a quite remarkable experience, if a little nerve-wracking. With the cool air blowing in your face and the bridge shuddering with the impact of the traffic, you need a good head for heights. However, the views of the Firth of Forth, its islands, the hills of Fife and surrounding countryside are spectacular. On a clear day you can see as far as Dunfermline. The Forth Road Bridge was opened in 1964 and at over a mile and a half long (2½ kilometres) (including the approach viaducts) it's one of the longest suspension bridges in the world.

Bus: 18, 20, 24, 29
Open: all the time

EXTRA . . . EXTRA . . . While walking across the bridge look to the Forth Rail Bridge which has been described as one of the greatest engineering feats in the world. Work began in 1883 and it took 5,000 men seven years working day and night to complete it. The total cost was over £3 million.

GREYFRIARS CHURCHYARD, Greyfriars Place, south end of George IV Bridge

A graveyard not to be missed! Greyfriars Churchyard is a beautiful spot to stop and munch a sandwich. There's plenty of grass to sit on and an excellent view of the castle. This quiet haven dotted with fascinating gravestones, including that of Jock Grey (*see Greyfriars Bobby, page*

47), and flanked by impressive 'tomb-rooms', was once a prison site where 1,000 Covenanters were held for five months in terrible conditions. (*See also Greyfriars Church, page 47*.)

Open: daily

EXTRA . . . EXTRA . . . Sir George Mackenzie, Lord Advocate, was responsible for the prosecution of the Covenanters. His zeal earned him the title 'Bluidy Mackenzie'.

HERMITAGE OF BRAID, The Hermitage Visitors Centre, Braid Road. Tel: 031-447 7145

One of the joys of walking through this mile-long wooded gorge, with the Braid Burn running gently through, is that there are so few prohibitive signs and you are free to wander where you like. Although the paths and walkways are well defined, you get the feeling that everything around has been left to grow in its natural state. To appreciate the park properly, it's a good idea to go on a guided walk which takes you through the Hermitage and Blackford Hill (*see page 13*). These walks, which last about an hour and a half, are organized at regular intervals throughout the summer and have a theme such as 'Local Wild Flowers' or 'Summer Flowers'. The meeting point is usually the Hermitage Visitor Centre.

The centre also organizes regular summer evening talks, and at weekends you can watch the two audiovisual presentations 'The Story of the Hermitage' and 'The Changing Seasons'. There's also a countryside ranger on duty who will answer your questions. For details of all the activities contact the above address.

The Hermitage Visitor Centre was opened in 1938, a gift from the late John McDougal to the people of the city of Edinburgh. He said that the house and grounds should be 'used as a Public Park and Recreation Ground for the benefit of Citizens'. The house was originally built for Charles Gordon of Cluny, father of the Countess of Stair (*see Lady Stair's House, page 94*) and completed in 1785. To the west of the house is a waterfall and nearby you'll see an old millstone. A cornmill used to stand here before Charles Gordon of Cluny bought the land and replaced the mill with trees. There are plenty of places for picnicking so it's well worth spending a whole day here.

Bus: 5, 11, 15, 16
Open: Park: all the time

   Centre: Monday–Thursday, 0900–1700; Sunday
   1200–1700

EXTRA . . . EXTRA . . . In the 12th century this area was noted for its castles, built by the famous Barons of Braid.

HOLYROOD PARK

Holyrood Park – just a short walk from the bottom of the Royal Mile (*see Walk 3,   page 147*) – is, considering its position in the centre of Edinburgh, a huge open space. It's an area of natural moorland scenery which provides an exhilarating contrast to the cramped quarters of the Old Town. The park includes Arthur's Seat (*see page 13*), Whinny Hill, Hunter's Bog and Salisbury Crags. It is circled by Queen's Drive which passes Dunsapie Loch and St Margaret's Loch. Just beside St Margaret's Loch you can see the ruins of St Anthony's Chapel which was associated with the cure of eye disease; so too was St Margaret's Well which is near the palace. The well is said to have been brought from Restalrig where the spring waters were thought to cure eye problems. But the real joy of Holyrood Park is the fresh air; so why not set out for a long walk – you won't be disappointed. Look out for rabbits, voles, shrews and foxes which all make their homes in the park's rough grassland. These grounds have inspired many great literary works including Sir Walter Scott's *Heart of Midlothian* which is mainly set here. And, as you walk, it's interesting to know that where you tread once formed part of the ancient sanctuary of Holyrood where anyone in financial difficulty could claim twenty-four hours' safety from their creditors.

Open: all the time

EXTRA . . . EXTRA . . . Salisbury Crags were quarried during the 19th century to provide paving slabs for Edinburgh's streets. Between 15 June 1815 and 4 June 1819, approximately 15,950 tons of rock were quarried for paving stones – and double that amount was taken for other purposes. Quarrying continued until 1831, and was halted only after the *Scotsman* newspaper (*see page 80*) had pleaded in its leading article that the destruction of 'the finest natural beauties, the richest ornaments, the noblest monuments in the place . . .' should be stopped.

LEITH LINKS

This public park, which covers 45 acres, is largely given over to sporting activities with a bowling green, tennis courts and pitches for rugby and football. However, it is most noted for its history as a golf course. It was here, on 7 March 1744, that the first rules of golf were recorded by 'gentlemen of honour skilfull in the ancient and healthful exercise of the golf', though the game had been played here for many years before. James I of England was keen on the game and played many a round at Leith Links; so too did Charles I who was in the middle of a game here in 1642 when he heard the news of the Irish rebellion. One of the most famous golf challenges was played by the Duke of York, the future James II of England, who partnered a local shoemaker called John Patterstone. They won, and their reward was so great that Patterstone could afford to build a house in Canongate. He named the house 'Golfer's Land' and put up a plaque, which still exists, with the motto 'Far and Sure'.

Bus: 12, 49
Open: all the time

EXTRA . . . EXTRA . . . Edinburgh is often called the 'Golf capital of the world': indeed, there are eighty-six courses within 20 miles of Princes Street.

LOCHEND PARK

This park always seems to be full of people – walkers, sunbathers, picnickers, children playing – and has a lively, busy atmosphere. Lochend Castle, built originally in the 16th century and occupied by the Logans of Restalrig, adds an historic air to the park, while the Lochend Loch makes it an ideal place for spotting some of Edinburgh's wildlife. Nearby is the famous Meadowbank Stadium, built for the 1970 Commonwealth Games and selected to play host to the 1986 Games. It's worth taking a walk around the grounds to see the sheer size of the stadium.

Bus: 13, 34, 35, 42
Open: all the time

EXTRA . . . EXTRA . . . Apparently the dovecote belonging to Lochend Castle was used for burning clothing and other items during the plague of 1645.

LONDON ROAD GARDENS, London Road

Sandwiched between Royal Terrace and London Road and very near the spectacular Calton Hill (*see page 17*), this strip of tree-filled parkland is popular with dog walkers. There are lots of trees here which are beautiful in the autumn, but the real reason to note this small park is that there are some free public toilets – there aren't many in Edinburgh, as you've probably already found out!

Open: all the time

EXTRA . . . EXTRA . . . Royal Terrace, built between 1821 and 1860, is the longest continuous frontage in the city – nearly a quarter of a mile!

THE MEADOWS, off Melville Drive

The best way to get to this park is by walking along the tree-lined Meadow Walk. It's the ideal place to rest your feet for a while, and has become a favourite haunt for university students who study while they sunbathe. It's also popular during the Festival (*see Edinburgh Festival Fringe, page 112*) when many major events are held here – some traditional, such as cricket matches, others more bizarre, such as pram races and sponsored three-legged walks.

Open: all the time

EXTRA . . . EXTRA . . . 'Under these trees', Lord Cockburn wrote of The Meadows, 'walked and talked and meditated all our literary and scientific worthies' – something to think about as you picnic in the shade.

PENTLAND HILLS

They're simply wonderful! The Pentlands are the nearest hills to Edinburgh on which you can do some real walking – so take stout shoes with you, you'll need them. The Pentlands can be spotted from many high points in Edinburgh (try Calton Hill, *see page 17*) and seem temptingly near. Indeed, they are just a short bus ride away so make sure you make the effort to walk them, if you're fit! There are excellent views and on a clear day you'll be able to make out many of Edinburgh's famous landmarks. However, the delight of the Pentland Hills is their feeling of open space; you may even catch sight of deer. You'll certainly be well out of the tourist crowds up here!

Bus: 9, 44, 45
Open: all the time

EXTRA . . . EXTRA . . . Balerno is a good place to end your walk over the Pentland Hills. There's a bus from here back to Edinburgh. The village seems to sprawl in a rather ugly way for several miles, but the buildings clustered round the local pub are well preserved and picturesque.

PRINCES STREET GARDENS

Right in the heart of Edinburgh, Princes Street Gardens is an excellent place in which to rest tired feet for a few minutes. Princes Street, which stretches along one side of the gardens, goes about its business while, high on its rock on the other side, is the omnipresent castle. Even the railway running through these well-laid-out flower-beds and lawns is an interesting feature. The iron bridge spanning the railway lines provides a popular and safe vantage point for train-spotting. (*See also Scott Monument, page 66.*)

Open: all day until dusk

EXTRA . . . EXTRA . . . The princess of Princes Street shops is Jenners, Edinburgh's answer to London's Harrods. Designed by William Hamilton Beattie and completed in 1895, Jenners is the last word in civilized good taste.

*ROYAL BOTANIC GARDEN, Inverleith Row

Edinburgh's Royal Botanic Garden, set in the grounds of the 19th-century Inverleith House, has become world famous for its work taxonomy, the classification of plants. Certainly, no one could dispute that they have an amazing variety to work on. The collection, which moved to its present site in 1830, was started as a 'physic garden' in

1670 on the site where Waverley Station now stands. It ranks second only to Oxford as the oldest botanic garden in Britain.

You'll need a good few hours and a pair of tough walking boots to explore the garden, and even then you'll want to come back. Whatever you do, don't miss the celebrated rock garden which covers 4 acres; the arboretum: the modern exhibition plant houses with their exotic displays; and the two palm houses. The larger, built in 1858, is the tallest greenhouse in Britain. There's also a fascinating exhibition hall full of interest for even the least green-fingered visitor. It's obviously best to visit in the summer months when the rhododendron walk is in its full glory, but there's plenty to see all year round and the garden leads on to Inverleith Park so you can extend your walk. The Royal Botanic Garden is also a haven for Edinburgh's wildlife with squirrels and many different birds including the kingfisher and water rail.

Bus: 23, 27
Open: Garden: summer, Monday–Saturday, 0900–one hour before sunset; Sunday, 1100
Winter, Monday–Saturday, 0900–dusk; Sunday, 1100

Plant houses: summer, Monday–Saturday, 1000–1700; Sunday, 1100
Winter, Monday–Saturday, 1000–1700 or dusk; Sunday, 1100

EXTRA . . . EXTRA . . . There's a memorial in the garden to Sir Carl Linnaeus, the 18th-century Swedish botanist who laid the foundation of modern day taxonomy.

SAUGHTON PARK, Balgreen Road

This park, to the west of Edinburgh, is only just beginning to gain much-deserved recognition as one of the city's more attractive open spaces.

The garden, planted by the Royal National Rose Society, is planned out in formal style, the varieties carefully identified and separated by ornately pruned hedges. In the summer, the display rose garden is a feast of colour. In the winter, the new winter garden (opened in September 1984) provides a welcome ray of light on a grim day – just the place to lift your spirits. There's also a dahlia garden and an Italian garden. With the Water of Leith running through the park, a number of much-used football pitches and some spectacular views of Edinburgh Castle, there's plenty going on here.

Bus: 12, 21, 38
Open: daily

EXTRA . . . EXTRA . . . There's a scented garden in the park, planted especially for blind people, with the names of the plants written in braille on plaques.

SLATEFORD TO COLINTON, Water of Leith

If you want to get away from the sights and the shops but don't want to get lost or exhausted, this walk beside the Water of Leith is the answer. Starting just behind the Dell Inn (if you're travelling by bus the driver will drop you off here), the walk looks a little uninspiring. Don't worry, it improves dramatically! Walk down the track beside the Inn, it will bring you quickly to the Water, and already things are looking better. In the early spring there are lots of snowdrops and primroses alongside the path which twists and turns with the Water. During the summer a sumptuous green canopy shades your route. When you reach a white house, cross the wooden bridge beside it and turn left. There are now a number of paths – make sure you keep to the lowest one wherever you can, it's much prettier. Eventually you will come to Colinton (*see page 125*) from where you can return to Edinburgh or continue to Juniper Green along a disused railway track.

Bus: 64, 65, 66
Open: all the time

EXTRA . . . EXTRA . . . Bonnie Prince Charlie stayed in Slateford, on 16 September 1745, when he arrived from Winchburgh and Kirkliston to demand the surrender of Edinburgh.

SPYLAW PARK

Very pretty and in a beautiful position beside the Water of Leith, Spylaw Park is well worth taking a look at if you're visiting Colinton (*see page 125*). Don't be put off by the entrance which is through rather private-looking gates marked 'Spylaw House'.

Bus: 16
Open: daily

EXTRA . . . EXTRA . . . There was once a snuff-mill behind and below Spylaw House, owned by James Gillespie who made his fortune from the milling. As you tour Edinburgh you may spot Gillespie Hospital and

James Gillespie's School – both endowed with money from the snuff!

UNION CANAL WALK

What better way to spend a sunny summer's day than walking along the canal? It's simply splendid – a mass of colourful wild flowers. But be warned, you need to dress sensibly as it gets a bit muddy at times and there's a lot of scrambling up and down to be done.

The canal was opened in 1822 to link Edinburgh with the Forth and Clyde Canal and transport heavy goods and passengers between Edinburgh and Glasgow. It's no longer used commercially but you'll see quite a few leisure boats idling up and down.

As you walk along the canal, notice the way it widens at certain points to form basins – stopping places where barges can turn, load and unload – and stop under the bridges to see the way the tow ropes of the barges have worn grooves in the corner stones. There are several places where you can join and leave the canal but the most central is at the old terminus at Fountainbridge, once known as Port Hopetoun. It's well worth taking your time and stopping frequently to enjoy the views, especially of the Pentland Hills (*see page 25*). And in case you want to measure your route, there are half-mile stones along the way!

Bus: 1, 30, 33, 34, 43
Open: all the time

EXTRA . . . EXTRA . . . The railway was opened in 1842, putting the canal out of business. At that time fares for a canalboat to take you from Edinburgh to Glasgow were between 4 and 6 shillings (20–30p) and the journey took between seven and a half and fourteen hours. The train cut the journey to two and a quarter hours and cost much the same.

WARRISTON CEMETERY, Warriston Road

Warriston, like Calton Burying Grounds (*see page 16*) and Greyfriars Churchyard (*see page 19*), is worth searching out. It rambles beside the Water of Leith over a large area on varying levels and is dotted with trees. There are so many gravestones – some in orderly rows, some randomly placed and some tumbling over – that they seem to form a forest of stone. Many of the stones are individually interesting but look out for the obelisk corner – you'll never see so many obelisks together again!

Bus: 34
Open: daily

EXTRA . . . EXTRA . . . You can get a good view of rugby matches at nearby George Heriot's Sports Ground by looking over the low wall near the Warriston Gardens exit of the cemetery.

ANCHOR CLOSE, High Street, off the Royal Mile

William Smellie's printing house used to stand in this close and it was here that he printed the first edition of *Encyclopaedia Britannica* in 1768 and the Edinburgh edition of the verses of Robert Burns in 1787. Burns used to come to read the proofs; he also did a fair amount of drinking in Anchor Close at Dawney Douglas's Anchor Tavern, home of the 'Crochallan Fencibles' drinking club. Burns's verses 'Rattlin' Roarin' Willie' were based on William Dunbar, lawyer and 'Colonel' of the club. (*See also Walk 3 The Royal Mile, page 147.*)

Open: all the time

EXTRA . . . EXTRA . . . Robert Burns was born on 25 January 1759 and Scots people celebrate that date with a traditional Burns supper of haggis, mashed tatties and neeps (potatoes and turnips), followed by kebbuck and bannocks (cheese and oatcakes).

BRODIE'S CLOSE, Lawnmarket, off the Royal Mile

Edinburgh can boast many notorious citizens but surely Deacon William Brodie, who lived in this close, must be one of the most fascinating character of all. He was a cabinet-maker and town councillor by day, and at night leader of a house-breaking gang! The turnpike stair on the right leads up to his house. Look at the huge lock, Brodie's own work. Deacon Brodie was eventually caught burgling the Excise Office in nearby Chessel's Court and was hanged in 1788 at a gallows he designed himself. His name lives on in the public house opposite, a 17th-century building which stands on the site of the gallows. (*See also Walk 3   The Royal Mile, page 147.*)

Open: all the time

EXTRA . . . EXTRA . . . Robert Louis Stevenson is thought to have based *Dr Jekyll and Mr Hyde* on Deacon Brodie.

BURNS MONUMENT, Regent Road

Scotland's most famous poet, Robert Burns, wrote of Edinburgh, 'Edina! Scotia's darling seat'. (*See also Anchor Close, page 35.*) The poet is remembered by a monument which is neither spectacular nor interesting and which is situated on a bleak spot overshadowed by Calton Hill (*see page 17*). However, there are excellent intimate views of both the Palace of Holyroodhouse (*see Holyrood Park, page 21*) and Arthur's Seat (*see page 13*). If you can admit to having a nosy interest in the way other people live, this is the spot to snoop from! The backs of terraced houses, offices, flats and churches all offer an unusual and alternative face of Edinburgh. There's also a handy route to the better-known parts of the capital down a steep path from the Burns Monument to Tolbooth Wynd and then to Canongate near the foot of the Royal Mile (*see also Walk 3, The Royal Mile, page 147*).

Open: all the time

EXTRA . . . EXTRA . . . A short walk from Burns Monument is the Old Royal High School. Among its former pupils were architect Robert Adam; pioneer of the telephone Alexander Graham Bell; and, perhaps most famous of all, Sir Walter Scott (*see Scott Monument, page 66*).

CANNONBALL HOUSE, Castle Hill, off the Royal Mile

Look at the west gable of this house, dated 1630, and you'll see a cannonball firmly embedded in the wall. Quite how or why it got there is the centre of many a Scottish controversy. Some say it was fired by Cromwell's troops, others during the blockade of the castle by Bonnie Prince Charlie in 1745. It is also reputed to be a marker for the gravitation height of the city's first water supply piped up from Comiston Springs into the Castle Hill Reservoir which stands opposite and is still in use. Go and see the cannonball and make up your own mind! (*See also Walk 3, page 147*).

Open: all the time

EXTRA . . . EXTRA . . . Across the street from Cannonball house, near Castle Wynd, there's a bronze plaque which records that this was where more than 300 'witches' were burned between 1479 and 1722.

CANONGATE KIRK, Canongate, off the Royal Mile

Built in basilica style, this church, 'the kirk in the Canongate, is uncharacteristic of Scottish Presbyterian churches. It was originally part of the Abbey of Holyrood, now in ruins, and served both as the parish church of Canongate and as the Chapel Royal where kings and queens of Scotland were baptized, married, crowned and buried. However, that all came to an end in 1688 when King James VII turned the Abbey Church into the Roman Catholic Chapel Royal.

This new church was built in 1688 with money left to the crown by a rich merchant, Thomas Moodie. His coat of arms is above the main entrance. There's lots of interest to see and the fact that it is newly decorated and obviously well-cared for makes browsing even more appealing. The Palace of Holyroodhouse (*see page 54*) and Edinburgh Castle (*see page 42*) are in the parish of Canongate, so the royal family attend services here when they're staying in Edinburgh: they have a special pew at the front of the centre aisle. Royal visits have been recorded by a collection of photographs displayed near the entrance to the church. (*See also Walk 3   The Royal Mile, page 147*.)

Open: to visit ask at the manse in Reid's Court near the church

---

EXTRA . . . EXTRA . . . The churchyard is well worth wandering around. Several people of note are buried here including Adam Smith, the economist who wrote *The Wealth of Nations*, and 'Clarinda', the special friend of Robert Burns.

CHARLOTTE BAPTIST CHAPEL, West Rose Street

This chapel, which stands at the Charlotte Square end of Rose Street, is deceptively large. Built in 1908 in the style of Wren, it has 1,000 seats and two halls. The best time to visit is on Sunday morning when you may find yourself joining in the service!

Open: daily

EXTRA . . . EXTRA . . . Alexander Graham Bell, inventor of the telephone, was born at 16 South Charlotte Street in 1876.

THE CHURCH OF ST ANDREW AND ST GEORGE, George Street

You can be assured of a warm welcome at this attractive 18th-century church, especially on a Sunday morning when a large congregation fills its pews. Known as 'The Church in the City', it is certainly in a prime position and was originally built as St Andrew's Church in 1782–4 as an integral part of James Craig's original New Town plan. St George's Church, now West Register House (*see page 108*), stood about half a mile to the west in Charlotte Square. However, the two congregations were united in 1964. The church is noted for its elliptical (almost oval) nave. Look up and you'll see the oval shape reflected in the ceiling pattern. The designer, Major Andrew Frazer, was particularly impressed by the Church of St Andrew in Via Quirinale in Rome and, as a tribute to St Andrew, patron saint of Scotland, used the unusual shape as a model for this church. The 167 foot (51m) high steeple was added in 1787. The undercroft is now a chapel, session room and very inviting café. (*See also Walk 4 New Town, page 151*).

Open: daily (undercroft weekdays 1200–1400)

EXTRA ... EXTRA ... Walk across St Andrew Square and look at no. 35 – the oldest house in the square. This used to be Douglas's Hotel and was patronized by such notables as Queen Victoria, Empress Eugénie, wife of Napoleon III, and Sir Walter Scott.

COLINTON CHURCH, Colinton

This is a beautiful church, not to be missed if you're visiting Colinton (*see page 125*) or walking the Water of Leith (*see Slateford to Colinton, page 28*). It's also featured on the Robert Louis Stevenson Heritage Trail (*see page 58*), as the novelist's grandfather, Dr Lewis Balfour, was once its minister. The extremely pretty and very well-kept churchyard is a peaceful spot in which to stop and contemplate the clear waters which run beside it.

Bus: 16
Open: daily

EXTRA ... EXTRA ... Look out for an old mort safe to the left of the entrance gates of the churchyard. It was used to keep graves safe from body-snatchers. (*See also St Cuthbert's Church, page 60.*)

CORSTORPHINE CHURCH, High Street, Corstorphine

Certainly worth visiting if you're in Corstorphine (*see page 125*), this attractive small church has many interesting relics. There's an effigy of Sir Adam Forester (d. 1405), an ancient font – thought to be as much as 1,000

years old – and many heraldic panels. Look out for the
hour-glass behind the pulpit – it was used for timing the
sermons!

Bus: 12, 31, 36
Open: daily 1030–1200 or by appointment: telephone
Corstorphine Trust Museum 031-334 4722

EXTRA . . . EXTRA . . . The electric light high on the
outside of the church has replaced a lamp which long ago
was lit at dark to guide travellers safely through the
marsh and along the loch edge.

DUDDINGSTON CHURCH, Old Church Lane, Duddingston

Duddingston Church is the oldest building in the village
(*see page 128*), dating back to the 12th century. It is
situated in a very picturesque spot beside Duddingston
Loch and should not be missed if you are in the area. In
the churchyard there is a tower built to guard against
body-snatchers, and near the gate there's an iron collar
and chain – which gives you some idea of the punishment
snatchers would get if caught.

Bus: 2, 21, 36, 42 to Holyrood Park Road, then 1 mile
(1½km) walk
Open: daily

EXTRA . . . EXTRA . . . Look out for the loupin-in-on
stone, used by riders if they needed help to mount their
horses.

DUGALD STEWART MEMORIAL, Calton Hill, nr Regent Road

This monument to Dugald Stewart, Professor of Philosophy at Edinburgh University (1786–1828), is a copy of the choragic monument of Lysicrates in Athens. As a leading philosopher of his day and author of *Philosophy of the Human Mind*, Stewart was named by his contemporaries 'the Bacon of Metaphysics'. (*See also Calton Hill, page 17.*)

Open: all the time

EXTRA . . . EXTRA . . . At the east corner of Calton Hill and Regent Road is Rock House, the home and studio of David Octavius Hill, pioneer portrait and landscape photographer.

EDINBURGH CASTLE, The Rock, off the Royal Mile

First, you *do* have to pay to go into the castle. However, as it dominates Edinburgh it can be clearly viewed from many parts of the city and from many of the surrounding hills (*see Walk 1   Floodlit Edinburgh, page 139; Calton Hill, page 17; Braid Hills, page 14; Blackford Hill, page 13*). Indeed, the most important point about the castle is its site and fortification – most of the buildings inside are rather disappointing.

The castle has served as a prison, an armoury and a palace, but high on its basalt rock 435 feet (133m) above sea level it was built as a fortress. Its present shape dates from the 14th century. In 1356 King David II built a 60 foot (18m) high tower on the site of what is now Half Moon

Battery (this can be seen from the eastern side of the castle). This fortification, which became known as David's Tower, withstood all attacks until the reign of Mary Queen of Scots. The castle was the last place to uphold Mary's cause and was held for the exiled Queen by Sir William Kircaldy. However, in 1573, surrounded and attacked by thirty cannons, David's Tower eventually collapsed. Kircaldy surrendered and was hanged and beheaded.

From 1649 to 1650 the castle was made more impregnable by removing the spur of land in front of it; Edinburgh citizens were used as forced labour for the task. Just over half a century later the Union of Parliaments in 1707 effectively meant that the castle was no longer needed as a military defence and it became a barracks and a prison. However, the connection between the military and the castle has survived – even though the castle is, today, a major tourist attraction. It remains the headquarters of the Royal Scots Guards, the Royal Scots Dragoon Guards and the Army School of Piping.

As mentioned, you can see much of the castle without entering its walls, but there *is* a small part which you are allowed to visit without charge – the war memorial. The Scottish National War Memorial commemorates the 150,000 Scots who died during World War I and is one of the most moving memorials to be seen anywhere. Another part of the castle which you can visit without paying a fee is the esplanade. It was built in 1753 as a parade ground and is now the site of Edinburgh's world famous, and very colourful, Military Tattoo (fee). From here you can get a good look at the Gatehouse with its crest of the Royal Arms of Scotland. It was built in 1887 as a symbolic entrance and is flanked by statues of Robert the Bruce and William Wallace which were added in 1929. Its retractable drawbridge was the last to be built in Scotland. The esplanade also provides a magnificent view of Edinburgh and it's easy, when surveying the city, to see why the castle was built on this particular spot. (*See also Beating the Retreat, page 113.*)

Open: Esplanade: April–September, Monday–Saturday 0930–1705; Sunday 1100–1705
October–March, Monday–Saturday 0930–1620; Sunday 1230–1535

Scottish National War Memorial: as above but by special permission only, write in advance or ask at ticket office

---

EXTRA ... EXTRA ... The name 'Castle Rock' comes from the time when a Saxon Queen, Margaret, wife of Malcolm III, decided to turn what was a very basic fortress into a palace. Malcolm, it's interesting to note, was the son of Duncan and successor to Macbeth.

ELIM PENTECOSTAL CHURCH, 26 George IV Bridge

If you're passing this 19th-century gothic-style church then do go in to see the John Knox pulpit – the only one still in use in Edinburgh. Knox (c. 1514–72), a leading figure in the Scottish Kirk, introduced the Protestant Reformation in Scotland. It's also of interest that this is one of only three churches in Edinburgh still offering full immersion baptism.

Open: daily

EXTRA ... EXTRA ... George IV Bridge, with Cowgate running below, was built in 1829–34 by Thomas

Hamilton to link the Old Town with the up-and-coming area of George Square.

FLODDEN WALL, the Vennel

You can still see the remains of Flodden Wall in the Vennel, a steep passageway leading up from the south-west corner of Grassmarket (*see page 46*). The wall was built in 1513 – a panic reaction to the Scottish defeat at the Battle of Flodden on 9 September 1513. This was the most bloody of all the Border conflicts and saw the death of James IV and thousands of his soldiers. However, as no invasion followed the wall became a boundary defining the official burgh limits of Edinburgh.

Open: all the time

EXTRA . . . EXTRA . . . Lady Carolina Nairne (1766–1845), writer of many popular Scottish songs, wrote these words after the tragic battle:

> I've heard them a'lilting, at the yowe milkin',
> Lassies a'liltin' afore dawn o' day,
> But noo they are moanin', on ilka green loanin',
> The Floo'ers o' the forest are a' wede awae.

GEORGE HERIOT'S SCHOOL, Lauriston Place

Although you can't actually go into the school, it's well worth taking a look at this impressive building from the outside and, if the gate is open, strolling through the grounds. Although the main entrance is in Lauriston

Place this is, in fact, the back of the building, to get a view of the front you'll need to go to the Castle Esplanade. It was designed in the style of Inigo Jones although the architect is not known, and was built between 1628 and 1660 with money left by George Heriot, a goldsmith and banker, nicknamed 'Jingling Geordie'. The school was taken over by Cromwell and used as a hospital after the Battle of Dunbar in 1650, but nine years later it reverted to a school and still has a very good reputation. A remarkable feature of the building is the windows, some 200 in number and each one different!

EXTRA . . . EXTRA . . . George Heriot became a favourite with James VI who used to rely on him for 'financial help' in his 'personal matters'.

GRASSMARKET

This square (or rectangle) has a fascinating and chequered history: first as the site of a monastery built for the Grey Friars in 1447, later as a marketplace, site of jousting tournaments and a favourite retreat for Burns, Wordsworth and other writers who enjoyed a drink in the old White Hart Inn. On a more grim note, Grassmarket is notorious as a place of public execution. The gallows stood at the east end from 1666 to 1784, and the site is now marked by a St Andrew's Cross set in cobblestones. This is where over 100 Covenanters were hanged (*see Greyfriars Church, page 47*).

Open: all the time

EXTRA . . . EXTRA . . . During the 18th century, Edinburgh was the scene of many a medicine show where miracle cures and exotic potions were demonstrated. One of the most notorious medicine men was 'Doctor' James Graham, born in Grassmarket in 1745. He believed that people should 'abstain totally from flesh and blood, from all liquors but cold water and fresh milk, and from all excessive sensual indulgence'. He grew more eccentric as the years went by – indeed, he even proposed building a house at the top of Arthur's Seat (*see page 13*) 'to experience the utmost degree of cold that the climate of Edinburgh had to offer'.

GREYFRIARS BOBBY, corner of George IV Bridge and Candlemaker Row

Bobby was a faithful Skye terrier who refused to leave the grave of his dead master, border shepherd Jock Grey. For fourteen years he was fed by the people of Edinburgh and when he died in 1872 he was buried beside his master in Greyfriars Churchyard (*see page 19*). Greyfriars Bobby, as he became known, is remembered by a small, rather insignificant statue – but it's a nice story!

Open: all the time

EXTRA . . . EXTRA . . . On the wall of the pub behind Greyfriars Bobby look out for a penny-farthing bicycle.

GREYFRIARS CHURCH, Candlemaker Row

Greyfriars has had a turbulent history – both the building itself and the events associated with it. It dates from the beginning of the 17th century but by the middle of that century all its interior furnishings had been destroyed and it had been turned into a barracks. In May 1718, gunpowder stored in a tower exploded, destroying both the tower and nearby bays . . . and so it went on. It was in Greyfriars in 1638 that the first signatures were placed on the National Covenant which, while protesting loyalty to the king, was uncompromisingly against his ecclesiastical policy for Scotland. The Covenanters took a solemn oath to resist the 'contrary errours and corruptions' of the Anglican faith imposed by Charles I. Much suffering was to follow (*see Greyfriars Churchyard, page 19; Grassmarket, page 46*). There are copies of the Covenanters' banners hanging above the pillars inside the church.

Open: Monday–Friday 10.00–17.00

EXTRA . . . EXTRA . . . Grey Friars were Dutch friars who wore grey robes. They established a monastery here in the 13th century. In 1562 Queen Mary granted the garden of Greyfriars Monastery to Edinburgh to be used to relieve the overfull churchyard of St Giles (*see page 62*).

LADY STAIR'S CLOSE, Lawnmarket

The main feature is Lady Stair's House (*see page 94*) but the close contains a great deal more of historic interest and is a fascinating place to look around. Blackie House, towards the back, was originally built in the 17th century but has been added to since. Below Lady Stair's House is the Assembly Hall of the General Assembly of the Church of Scotland (*see page 18*) which is often used by theatrical groups during the Festival. Although they have now been demolished, other notable buildings in the close included the house where Robert Burns first stayed in Edinburgh and a tavern which was the scene of a notorious dinner for beggars hosted by essayist Sir Richard Steele in 1717. (*See also Walk 3   The Royal Mile, page 147.*)

Open: all the time

EXTRA . . . EXTRA . . . Lady Stair's Close was once the main access route between the Old Town and the New Town.

LAMB'S HOUSE, Water's Close, Burgess Street, Leith. Tel: 031-554 3131

Restored by the National Trust for Scotland, this four-storey, 17th-century merchant's house is now a day-centre for old people. Likely as not, you'll walk in on a game of bingo or a sing-song, so join in – everyone's welcome! Report at the reception desk first, then you're free to wander around. Look out especially for the huge stone fireplaces. Outside there's a pleasant garden where passers-by can rest weary feet. This garden used to stretch right down to the water.

Open: Monday–Friday, 0900–1700

EXTRA . . . EXTRA . . . The house was built for Andrew Lamb, a wealthy merchant and friend of Mary Queen of Scots. Apparently, she often visited the house on her way to the Highlands.

THE MAGDALEN CHAPEL, Cowgate

This 16th-century chapel, hidden behind railings, is one of the few remaining pre-Reformation church buildings in Edinburgh. The stained glass windows, one of the main features, are still intact. Look to the top right-hand window and you'll see the coat of arms of Mary of Lorraine, who was Queen Regent when the chapel was first dedicated. You can pick up a leaflet outlining its history and points of interest, such as the inscriptions round the north and east walls with the names, descriptions and trades of all the people who have given charitable gifts.

The chapel is used by the Heriot-Watt University as its Chaplaincy Centre and, as it has such good acoustics, the Music Society holds lunch-time concerts, usually on Wednesdays.

Open: to visit ask at the Scottish Reformation Society, 17 George IV Bridge. Tel: 031-225 1836

EXTRA . . . EXTRA . . . The chapel was once used as a mortuary and the old table now on the platform was the mortuary table. Situated so close to Grassmarket, the place of public execution, this was the ideal place to dress the dead for burial. The executed Covenanters (*see Grassmarket, page 46*) were buried here; so too was the Earl of Argyle.

MERCAT CROSS, High Street, off The Royal Mile

Situated in front of Parliament Hall (*see page 55*), Mercat Cross marks the spot where merchants once gathered to do business. The original medieval cross was demolished in 1756, the present one was restored by W. E. Gladstone in 1885. However, its shaft does contain a fragment of the ancient monument. Royal Proclamations are still heard from Mercat Cross, the platform from where the Battle of Flodden and the death of James IV were announced. And it's here that huge crowds gathered in 1745 to hear Prince Charles Edward proclaim his exiled father King James III. (*See also Walk 3 The Royal Mile, page 147.*)

Open: all the time

EXTRA . . . EXTRA . . . In *Marmion* Sir Walter Scott described how unearthly figures were seen over Edinburgh and a dreadful voice rang out from Mercat Cross naming those doomed to die in the coming battle.

NATIONAL MONUMENT, Calton Hill, off Regent Road

A prominent feature of Calton Hill (*see page 17*), National Monument was intended as a memorial to the Scottish soldiers and sailors who died during the Napoleonic wars. Designed to be an exact copy of the Parthenon in Athens, building work began in 1824 but funds, which were raised by subscription, ran out and the monument was never completed. Today the massive Doric columns have become known both as 'Scotland's pride and poverty' and 'Edinburgh's disgrace'.

Open: all the time

EXTRA . . . EXTRA . . . Nearby Regent Terrace has been home for a large number of notable people. They include: painter, engraver and founder of the Royal Academy, William Lazars; geographer, Henry Yule; and Milton's biographer David Masson. Masson lived at no.

10 and was frequently visited there by his friends Dickens and Carlyle.

NELSON MONUMENT, Calton Hill, off Regent Road

Think of an upturned telescope – now you know what Nelson Monument looks like! There's a fee to enter this 102 foot (31m) tower on Calton Hill (*see page 17*), so stay outside and look. You'll be able to see the battlement base and a sculpture representing the stern of Nelson's ship the *San Joseph* above its doorway. On the top there's a time-ball which drops daily at 1300 hours, the 'One O'clock' gun. (*See also National Monument, page 51; Dugald Stewart Memorial, page 42.*)

Open: all the time (to look from the outside)

EXTRA . . . EXTRA . . . Near Nelson Monument is a building known as the Observatory which was built in 1818; it stands by the Old Observatory which dates from 1776.

NICHOLSON SQUARE METHODIST CHURCH, Nicholson Square

Set back from the road with its own forecourt, the entrance to this early 19th-century church, designed by Thomas Brown, is impressive. Inside, it's all very simple, pristine and functional. The Gothic oak pulpit was brought from the now disused Lady Glenarchy's Church, Roxburgh Place, in 1974. If you want to walk around ask at the main office adjacent to the main door.

Open: daily

EXTRA . . . EXTRA . . . Beside the church are the Epworth Halls, now a meeting place for NACRO (National Association for the Care and Rehabilitaton of Offenders). They're open from Monday to Friday, 1000–1600, as a café serving excellent snacks and everyone is welcome.

OLD COLLEGE, corner of Chambers Street and South Bridge. Tel: 031-667 1011 ex 4444

Proposals to found 'ane universite' were being made at the beginning of the 16th century and by 1583 the first students of Arts and Divinity were enrolled. The building known today as Old College in fact dates from the 18th century. Designed by Robert Adam, the foundation stone was laid in 1789 by the Lord Provost. But it was completed much later during the 1820s by William Playfair: the Upper Library Hall (*see page 67*) is one of Playfair's best pieces of work. A visit to Old College today can seem quite formal, but that's part of its charm. Portraits of college principals, long dead, line the corridors. Look out for the Joseph Lister Collection: bequeathed to the university by his family, it's an impressive array of medals and titles including the Freedom of the City of London.

Open: 0900–1600. Telephone for an appointment or go to the reception desk and ask to be shown round (this might not be possible if it's in use)

EXTRA . . . EXTRA . . . Studying was tough in the early days of the university. 'Dictates' were given every day from 5 A.M. until the evening with only one break –

for compulsory exercise. Students were forbidden to attend the very popular public executions which were thought to be too frivolous!

PALACE OF HOLYROODHOUSE, Abbey Strand, off the Royal Mile

You do have to pay to go inside but there's nothing to stop you enjoying the palace from the outside, and no visit to Edinburgh would be complete without spending at least a few minutes gazing up at a building so crammed with Scottish history. It really is magnificent: first the wrought-iron gates, built in 1922 as part of a national memorial to Edward VII, then the courtyard with the fountain at the centre, and finally the palace itself – built in the style of Louis XIV with an entrance of Doric columns. Work began on the palace in 1498 during James IV's reign. It was built as an extension of an existing guesthouse belonging to the old abbey (now in ruins) which was founded in 1128.

The palace, now the official residence of the Queen and other members of the Royal Family during visits to the city, and of the Lord High Commissioner during the General Assembly of the Church of Scotland (*see page 118*), is probably best known as the home of the Catholic Mary Queen of Scots from 1561 to 1567 and the scene of the infamous murder of her favourite, Italian secretary David Rizzio. He was so hated by Protestant militants that they left fifty-six dagger wounds in his body. It was also at the palace that James VI learned that he was to be James I of England. Apparently a messenger rode all the way – some 400 miles – from Elizabeth I's death-bed in Richmond Palace, Surrey to the Palace of Holyroodhouse in only sixty-two hours. (*See also Walk 2, page 143; Walk 3, page 147.*)

EXTRA . . . EXTRA . . . Legend has it that the original abbey from which the palace gets its name was built by David I on the site of his miraculous escape from death. He was out riding on a holy day – a forbidden practice – when he was attacked by a stag. He took the stag's antlers in his hands but as he did so the stag disappeared and he was left holding a Holy Cross or Rood.

PARLIAMENT HALL, Parliament Square

Completed in 1639 and the seat of Scottish Parliament until 1707 when the governments of Scotland and England were united, this is a really impressive hall. It has a wonderful hammer-beam roof, colourful hand-painted glass windows and a good collection of paintings by Raeburn and other major Scottish artists. One painting, on the wall opposite the main entrance, shows how law was once conducted here. The conditions, which were very cramped, completely lacked privacy. Lawyers and council had to walk up and down to avoid being over-heard. When you visit Parliament Hall you're almost certain to catch sight of members of the legal profession doing much the same today. Look out too for the oldest lead equestrian statue in Britain, erected in 1688, of Charles II. There's also a figure of John Knox and an interesting statue of Sir Walter Scott. The statue of Scott is said to be the best likeness of him in existence; it was carved in 1830 from sandstone by John Greenshields, a self-taught Lanarkshire sculptor.

Open: Tuesday–Friday, 1000–1600

EXTRA . . . EXTRA . . . Before Parliament Hall was built, the Scottish Parliament met in Edinburgh Castle (*see page 42*). They gathered in the great hall which was built by the Stewarts and is recorded in the Exchequer Rolls for 1433–4.

PATRICK GEDDES HERITAGE TRAIL

'Edinburgh's greatest all-round citizen' is how Patrick Geddes was once described, and if you follow this walk tracing his achievements you'll soon realize just how much he deserved the title. Patrick Geddes (1854–1932) spent ten years of his much-travelled life working as a Demonstrator of Botany at Edinburgh University, and from then on made Edinburgh his base. His life's work was to encourage the restoration and development of the slum areas in the city centre to make it a more pleasant place for people to live. He is also noted for setting up the Outlook Tower in 1882 (this is still open to the public as the Outlook Tower and Camera Obscura on Castle Hill, but there is an admission charge). The walk which starts at Mount Place and finishes at Queen's Drive is only a mile long, but it's worth taking your time to explore the area. You can pick up a leaflet called 'Patrick Geddes Heritage Trail' free from the Tourist Information Centre (Tel: 031-557 2727). This explains in detail the importance of each of the nineteen stops on the route.

Open: all the time

EXTRA . . . EXTRA . . . Geddes's motto was *'Vivendo Discimus'* which means 'By Living We Learn' and this is inscribed over the archway into the inner court of Riddle's

Close in the High Street (*see page below*). (*See also Walk 3 The Royal Mile, page 147.*)

RAMSAY LANE, Castle Hill, off the Royal Mile

This steep lane leading off Castle Hill is named after the 18th-century poet and author of *The Gentle Shepherd*, Allan Ramsay. He lived in a strangely shaped octagonal house known to locals as 'Goose-pie', and opened a bookshop nearby. The house still stands although it is rather overshadowed by other buildings – most notably Ramsay Gardens, built by Patrick Geddes (*see Patrick Geddes Heritage Trail, page 56*). Look at the roofline and you'll see a carving of a devil – still distinguishable although the weather has taken its toll. (*See also Walk 3 The Royal Mile, page 147.*)

Open: all the time

EXTRA . . . EXTRA . . . Ramsay, who originally came from Lanarkshire, spent much of his life trying to set up a legal theatre in Edinburgh – a project not approved of by the Catholic Church.

RIDDLE'S CLOSE, Lawnmarket, off the Royal Mile

This picturesque little close was the home of David Hume while he was writing his *History of Great Britain*. It's also known as 'MacMorran's Lodging'. Bailie John Mac-Morren, a wealthy citizen, lived in the 16th-century house in the inner court. He was shot dead in 1595 by a student of the Royal High School furious because MacMorran refused to grant an extra holiday. The house, now an adult education centre, was also the scene of a sumptuous banquet given by the city to James VI and Queen Anne of Denmark in 1598. (*See also Walk 3   The Royal Mile, page 147*.)

Open: all the time

EXTRA . . . EXTRA . . . Riddle's Close was restored by Patrick Geddes (*see Patrick Geddes Heritage Trail, page 56*) in 1889 and the houses were opened as the first halls of residence for students of the university.

ROBERT LOUIS STEVENSON HERITAGE TRAIL

This is an unusual but really rewarding way to explore Edinburgh and some of the surrounding villages. Robert Louis Stevenson (1850–94), author of, among other works, *Treasure Island* and *The Master of Ballantrae*, was born in Edinburgh at 8 Howard Place and spent much of his life in and around the city.

The trail starts at Lady Stair's House (*see page 94*), where there is an exhibition of Stevenson mementoes, and takes you through the New Town where he grew up, to the beautiful villages of Colinton, where he stayed with his maternal grandmother in Colinton Manse in the 1850s (*see page 125*), and Swanston, one of his favourite holiday homes (*see page 136*). The trail then goes over his best-loved stomping ground, those 'hills of home', the Pentland Hills (*see page 25*); to South Queensferry (*see page 133*) where the Hawes Inn, mentioned in *Kidnapped*, still stands; and to other spots associated with Stevenson. It's not the kind of tour you can do in a day, unless you have a fast car! Instead, take each part separately and enjoy putting all the pieces of the literary jigsaw together. You can pick up a leaflet describing the trail with a route map from either the Tourist Information Centre (Tel: 031-557 2727) or from Lady Stair's House.

EXTRA . . . EXTRA . . . Stevenson died at the age of only forty-four – he was a man of poor health. Much as he loved Edinburgh, he was for ever complaining about the chilly winds and described North Bridge as 'that windiest spot, or high altar, in this Northern temple of winds'.

ROMAN FORT, Cramond

Excavations in Cramond (*see page 126*) from 1954 to 1966 revealed the outline of a Roman fort some 540 feet by 460 feet (165 by 140m). The settlement, part of the Antonine Wall (which stretched between Forth and Clyde), was defended by a clay rampart 23 feet (7m) thick. Cramond's Parish Church is partly situated on the principia (the Roman headquarters) and next to it you can see a plan of the fort. The plan itself is made from Roman stones while coins and artefacts found on the site are in Huntly House (*see page 92*).

Bus: 4, 9, 10
Open: all the time

EXTRA . . . EXTRA . . . Cramond originates from Fort on the Almond.

ROYAL BANK OF SCOTLAND, Dundas House, 36 St Andrew Square

This Georgian building seems totally at odds with the rest of the architecture of the New Town as it is the only one set back from the road. Indeed, it doesn't fit into the original redevelopment scheme, designed by James Craig, at all. The site was intended for a church, but Sir Laurence Dundas, a wealthy Member of Parliament, used his influence to buy the land in 1772 and built his town house on it. It was taken over by the Royal Bank of Scotland in 1825 and the new banking hall added in 1858. Even if you don't need to use the banking facilities it's worth taking a look inside this hall with the splendid star-detailed dome.

You can pick up a free leaflet about Dundas House and also a free picture postcard at the reception desk.

Open: Monday–Friday, 0930–1530

EXTRA . . . EXTRA . . . As you look towards the building, you'll see a small sentry box to the left. This was erected in 1831 to defend the Bank 'against threat of outrages from Mobs' during the build-up to the Great Reform Act of 1832.

ST CUTHBERT'S CHURCH, Lothian Road

The original church on the site of St Cuthbert's was built over 1,000 years ago. Details are blurred but it was probably a Culdee Settlement of the Celtic Church. The present 19th-century building designed by Hippolyte Blanc retains an 18th-century tower. The simple grey internal walls make an effective contrast to the stained glass windows – all but one of which were designed and made locally. Above the altar there is an impressive dome (for a good view go up into the gallery) while behind it is an alabaster frieze of Leonardo da Vinci's 'Last Supper'. The most interesting part of St Cuthbert's is perhaps the tiny, very pretty War Memorial Chapel (1914–18). Beneath a barrelled ceiling in the base of the 18th-century tower, marble panels 'honour those who fell in the war'. Stark lettering in lead records just five names on each panel. They are in 'alphabetical order without distinction of rank. Their sacrifice and the honour due to them is the same.'

Open: daily

EXTRA . . . EXTRA . . . The notorious pair Burke and Hare, body-snatchers, were in a grisly business – providing bodies for medical students. They started their macabre activities by snatching corpses fresh from their graves. Eventually, running out of graves to plunder, they turned to murder. To soak up the atmosphere, take a walk round St Cuthbert's graveyard at dusk . . .

ST GEORGE'S WEST CHURCH, corner of Stafford Street and Shandwick Place. Tel: 031-225 7001

St George's West was the outcome of a remarkable struggle among Scotland's churches. In 1843 the minister of St George's in Charlotte Square, now West Register House (*see page 108*), Dr R. S. Candlish, along with hundreds of other ministers, left the Established Church to found the Free Church of Scotland. Many of his congregation followed him and became popularly known as the congregation of Free St George's. The 'West' part of the name came much later when, in 1929, it was added to distinguish it from the Charlotte Square church. Today St George's West has developed from being simply a place of worship into something more like a community centre with a friendly tea-room. The church itself is well worth taking a look at as an example of the severe Presbyterian style. Originally all symbolism was strictly avoided, but more recently crosses have been introduced.

Open: daily. Church centre and tea-room: Monday–Friday, 1200–1400

Church Office: Monday–Friday, 0930-1230, 1400–1630

EXTRA . . . EXTRA . . . In 1900 the United Presbyterian Church formed a union with the Free Church of Scotland. A minority of the Free Church was opposed to the union and continued as the Free Church of Scotland – they were nicknamed the 'Wee Frees'.

---

*ST GILES' CATHEDRAL (The High Kirk of St Giles), High Street, off the Royal Mile

St Giles' Cathedral is a must on any visit to Edinburgh, and as it's on the Royal Mile (*see Walk 3, page 147*) it's easy to include on even the shortest of visits. There has been a church on this site since A.D. 854 but most of the present building dates from 1829, with only the tower being from the 15th century. It was a cathedral for only five years, following the introduction by Charles I of bishops to the Presbyterian Church. There are lovely stained glass windows by the Pre-Raphaelite Edward Burne-Jones. Commemorated in St Giles' are the 1st Marquis of Montrose and the 1st Marquis of Argyll – bitter enemies until the very end of their lives, when both were executed.

Open: daily: January–March 0900–1700
April–September 0900–1900

EXTRA . . . EXTRA . . . Decorative cobbles outside St Giles' Cathedral are known as the Heart of Midlothian. They mark the site of the Old Tolbooth which was stormed during the Porteous Riots of 1736. Captain Porteous was condemned to death for ordering his troops to fire into a crowd which had refused to disperse. When a reprieve was sent from London an incensed mob took justice into their own hands and hanged Porteous. Scott based *Heart of Midlothian* on these violent events.

ST JOHN'S CHURCH, Princes Street

St John's, at the west end of Princes Street, is an impressive 19th-century church built between 1815 and 1818. It is buttressed in the Gothic tradition, with soaring pinnacles and beautiful 'mosaic' stained glass windows. It is a good idea to combine a visit to St John's with a tour of St Cuthbert's (*see page 60*) which is just behind – there's quite a contrast.

Open: daily

EXTRA . . . EXTRA . . . Take a walk round St John's churchyard; its walled terraces hide secluded benches. Look out for the memorial to Dean Ramsay – a granite cross some 24 feet (7.3m) high.

ST MARK'S UNITARIAN CHURCH, Castle Terrace

Although the actual church was founded in 1776, it wasn't until 1835 that the congregation moved to this building designed by David Bryce. Built in the shadow of the overpowering Castle Rock, the special feature of the church is the exterior with its Italian-style details and Doric doorway. Inside it is rather stark and modern although the organ, dated 1911, still looks magnificent.

Open: daily

EXTRA . . . EXTRA . . . David Bryce (1803–76) was a leading architect in Edinburgh. Among other buildings he worked on were The Royal Bank of Scotland (*see page 59*), Greyfriars Church (*see page 47*) and St George's West Church (*see page 61*).

ST MARY'S CATHEDRAL (Episcopal), Palmerston Place

St Mary's was the first cathedral erected in Britain after the Reformation. Its architect, George Gilbert Scott, set about re-creating an authentic Gothic style – and the result is impressive. Which is just as well because Scott had high hopes for his cathedral; when describing how he created its design he said: 'I have myself been most impressed by the earlier phase of the early pointed period, which especially unites the architecture of Scotland and Northern England, and is capable of the greatest possible degree of dignity, united with a remarkable amount of simplicity and any amount of beauty.'

Well, did he succeed? Judge for yourself! You enter St Mary's through a west-facing door beneath an impressive carved stone archway, a variant of that at Holyrood. It's interesting to note that Scott was aware that the site for the cathedral was once owned by the Abbey of Holy Rood (*see The Palace of Holyroodhouse, page 54*). Make sure you take a look at the wrought-iron screens made in 1879 by Skidmore. They're based on medieval designs from the *Book of Hours*. When you've seen all you want to see inside, visit St Mary's Music School (you can only look from outside) – a picturesque cluster of turrets and gables to the north of the cathedral.

Open: daily

EXTRA . . . EXTRA . . . During the 17th century the land on which St Mary's is built belonged to wealthy families living along the Royal Mile (*see Walk 3, page 147*) and was a favoured spot for their country homes.

ST MICHAEL'S, Inveresk

The first church of St Michael in Inveresk (*see page 129*) would probably have been made from mud and wattle, as early references date back as far as the 7th century. The present building, dating from 1806, is rather more substantial. There's something odd about the windows, though. Those down the right-hand side have typical Victorian stained glass while those down the left-hand side have clear glass. This was so that the fishermen sitting in the upper gallery, or Fishmen's Loft, could keep an eye on their boats – well that's the story!

Bus: 131
Open: daily

EXTRA . . . EXTRA . . . Next to the church is Inveresk House where Oliver Cromwell stayed for a night during his campaign in Scotland; his Roundheads stabled their horses in the church. In 1790 some alterations were made to Inveresk House during which a secret passage was discovered. The passage ended under the room where Cromwell slept and in it was found a skeleton in Cavalier dress. Beside the skeleton there was a full keg of gunpowder . . .

SCOTT MONUMENT, East Princes Street Gardens

You will be charged a fee to climb the 200 foot (60m) spire of this prominent monument in Princes Street Gardens (*see page 26*) but there's plenty to look at from ground level! The exterior is intricately decorated with sixty-four characters from Scott's novels and sixteen statuettes of Scottish poets. It's a real piece of Gothic fantasy. Designed by George Meikle Kemp, a joiner and craftsman, the tower is quite a contrast to the seated sculpted figure of Scott and his dog by Sir John Steell, over which it forms a canopy.

Open: daily – to look if not to climb!

EXTRA . . . EXTRA . . . The competition to design the Scott Monument was fierce and when Kemp won there was enormous controversy. He was both unknown and of 'lower' class. What's more, he'd beaten such highly-regarded architects as William Playfair (*see Upper Library Hall, page 67*).

SOUTH LEITH CHURCH, Kirkgate, Leith

The plaque outside this charming parish church gives 1483 as the date it was built and dedicated to St Mary.

But if you take a walk around the church and the churchyard, you'll see a lot has happened since then – it was badly damaged in the Siege of Leith in 1560, used by Cromwell's troops as an arms store from 1650 to 1657 and then completely restored in 1848. The church as it stands today was designed by Thomas Hamilton using St Isaac's, Leningrad, as a model.

It's a most interesting place to wander around – with all sorts of stones, inscriptions, monuments, epitaphs and burial arcades. Look out for the gravestones of the Balfours of Pilrig House, ancestors of Robert Louis Stevenson, and the Bartons, famous 15th-century sailors from Leith.

Bus: 10, 12, 16, 17, 22, 25, 37, 49
Open: daily

EXTRA . . . EXTRA . . . The church obviously found favour with James III – in 1487 he gave the generous sum of eight shillings (40p) to 'the new Kyrk of Leith to Our Ladie'.

UPPER LIBRARY HALL, Old College, corner of Chambers Street and South Bridge. Tel: 031-667 1011 ex 4444

Upper Library Hall is William Playfair's most distinctive contribution to designs for Old College (*see page 53*) by Robert Adam. It's a really superb room – 190 foot (58m) long, 50 foot (15m) wide and 40 foot (12m) high. In it are Sir Walter Scott's library table and Napoleon's dining table – spot the cigar burn!

Open: telephone to make an appointment to be shown around

EXTRA . . . EXTRA . . . Famous students of the university have included Lord Palmerston, Thomas Carlyle, Charles Darwin, Sir Arthur Conan Doyle, Oliver Goldsmith and Robert Louis Stevenson.

WHITE HORSE CLOSE, High Street, off the Royal Mile

Although this close, at the foot of Canongate, was redeveloped as private houses in 1965, it is still full of 17th-century character and interest. It was once a regular coaching stop with travellers staying the night in the White Horse Inn. In fact, it was from here that one of the first coaching services to England began. As the yard is so near to the Palace of Holyroodhouse, it's thought that it was once the site of the old stables and was named after Mary Queen of Scots' special steed. Another equestrian connection is William Dick's forge which he set up in the close in the 19th century. He was a famous farrier who founded the Royal Dick Veterinary College. All in all, this little close is steeped in history. (*See also Walk 3 The Royal Mile, page 147.*)

Open: all the time

EXTRA . . . EXTRA . . . In 1745, when Prince Charles Edward, the Young Pretender, occupied Edinburgh, the close was used as Jacobite headquarters.

CHAPTER THREE
People at Work

AIRPORT: EDINBURGH AIRPORT, Tel: 031-333 1000

Some seven miles west of the city centre, Edinburgh Airport is well worth a visit. There's lots to see and enthusiasts spend a whole day here plane-spotting. If the weather's fine, the high-level spectators' gallery provides an excellent view; if the weather's poor, then there are plenty of other places from which to watch the planes, large and small, taxi along the 8,400 foot (2,560m) runway. The runway became operational in 1976 and was part of a £15 million building programme which includes a bookshop, information desks and snack bars.

Open: all the time

EXTRA . . . EXTRA . . . Edinburgh Airport began its life as Turnhouse Aerodrome. It was created by the Royal Flying Corps in World War I because the nearby railway line could be used to deliver the planes. These early flying-machines were very primitive – they were delivered in pieces and then assembled on site.

AUCTIONS

Oil paintings, silver, coins and medals, musical instruments, furniture and carpets . . . they all come under the hammer at Edinburgh's two leading auction rooms –

Phillips, and Lyon and Turnbull. Everyone is welcome at their sales, either to buy or simply to watch the dealers in action. You'll soon spot the serious buyers who seem to have a sixth sense about exactly how much each item is worth. It can be a little confusing at first, but the staff are helpful and will explain what's going on. The various sales are held on different days and it's a good idea to telephone first so you can choose the one you find the most interesting. Alternatively, look in *The Scotsman*(*see Newspaper page 80*) on Saturday for a weekly list of sales.

Addresses: Phillips, 65 George Street. Tel: 031-225 2266

Lyon and Turnbull, 51 George Street. Tel: 031-225 4627

EXTRA . . . EXTRA . . . Nearby, at 13 Castle Street, there's a plaque marking the birthplace, in 1859, of author Kenneth Grahame who wrote *The Golden Age* and *The Wind in the Willows.*

BREWERY: NEW FOUNTAIN BREWERY, Gilmore Park

Home brewers, be prepared for a shock! At the New Fountain Brewery, part of the Scottish and Newcastle Breweries group, it's beer at the touch of a button. Although they've been brewing beer on this site since 1856 when the master brewer, William McEwan, first set up his own business, this new brewery was opened as recently as 1973 and automation is definitely the name of the game. Indeed, it has two of the fastest and most advanced canning lines in the world which, at peak production, turn out 1.8 million cans a day.

The tour, which lasts about an hour and a half, begins with an introductory film and then a guide takes you around the brewery answering questions as you go. You can see exactly how the beer and lager is brewed: from the 'mash' to the 'wort', from the fermenting vessels to the casks or the maturation vessels, and through the filter plant when it's ready for kegging, bottling or canning . . . and finally, for drinking. The tour ends with a glass or two of free beer, lager or a soft drink and a chance to chat to fellow-tourers.

Bus: 1, 30, 34, 35, 43
Open: Tours Monday–Thursday, from 1430. Book in advance by contacting Chief Brewery Guide, New Fountain Brewery, Gilmore Park, Edinburgh. Tel: 031-229 9377 ex 3015

EXTRA . . . EXTRA . . . One of the questions most often asked is about the difference between beer and lager. The word 'lager' is German for 'storage'. A special ycast is used and, after fermentation, the lager is stored (lagered) for a long period at low temperatures.

CRAFT: CELTIC CRAFT CENTRE, Paisley Close, 93–101 High Street, off the Royal Mile. Tel: 031-556 3228

The sound of bagpipes lures you into this craft centre tucked away in Paisley Close. From the outside it looks rather touristy, but inside the workers and assistants are helpful and proud of their high standard of workmanship. Here you can see kilt-makers, silversmiths and bagpipe-makers all engaged in making the various parts of the traditional Scottish dress – and that includes sporrans, swords, *sgian dhus* and dirks. If you're not sure what they are – the tartan-clad assistants will explain.

Open: Monday–Saturday, 0900–1730; Sunday, 1000–1730

EXTRA . . . EXTRA . . . A carving above the entrance to Paisley Close shows the head of twelve-year-old Joseph MacIvor with the inscription 'Heave awa' chaps, I'm no' dead yet!' This commemorates the disaster of 1816 when, at 1.00 A.M. on a Sunday morning, the building collapsed killing thirty-five people. Just as the rescuers had decided to call a halt to the search until the morning, a little voice called out, and Joseph was found amid the rubble.

---

*CRAFT: SCOTTISH CRAFT CENTRE, 140 Canongate, off the Royal Mile. Tel: 031-556 8136/7370

This is *the* place to buy your souvenirs – but don't worry, you don't have to buy to enjoy the Scottish Craft Centre. The works displayed here represent the very highest quality Scottish crafts and the choice is extremely wide-ranging. Glass, ceramics, leather work, tapestry, candles, jewellery, silversmithing, enamelling – you'll be able to see almost every type of craft exhibited here. If you're lucky you may even see someone working at their particular skill – perhaps firing a kiln in the garden. Have a chat, they're always very pleased to explain what they're doing.

Open: Monday–Saturday, 1000–1730

EXTRA . . . EXTRA . . . The craft centre is in 17th-century Acheson House – a good example of Scottish domestic architecture.

CRAFT: TEXTILE WORKSHOP AND GALLERY, Gladstone's Land, Lawnmarket, off the Royal Mile. Tel: 031-225 4570

It's a long climb up the turnpike stair to the workshop and gallery on the third floor of the 17th-century house, but if you're a keen needleperson then it's well worth the haul. Craftspeople are always at work at sewing and knitting machines, and there are special demonstrations from time to time of crafts such as spinning and weaving. Exhibitions of craftwork are held on a fairly regular basis – all, as you would imagine, of an extremely high quality. And if you're feeling inspired you can take a look at both craft materials and the finished articles for sale in the shop.

Open: April–October, Monday–Saturday, 1000–1700
            November–March, Tuesday–Saturday, 1000–1630

EXTRA . . . EXTRA . . . Gladstone's Land, a six-storey tenement house, was built for Thomas Gledstanes, an Edinburgh burgess, and completed in 1620.

DOCKS: LEITH DOCKS, Tower Place, Leith

Although cruise liners often call at the port of Leith for holiday-makers to step on to dry land and enjoy the sights of Edinburgh, it's important to remember that this is very much a working port, handling an estimated two million tons of cargo a year. With heavy loads and working machinery, there's action everywhere. A visit to the docks is a fascinating experience. You'll be amazed at the size of the ships which arrive and depart from places such as Holland, France, central America and the Middle

East. Recently, the port has concentrated on bulk grain importing but cargoes include a whole range of goods including coal and coke, petroleum products, chemical fertilizers and beer. The speed and efficiency with which it is all loaded and unloaded is quite remarkable – although machines have largely taken the place of muscle these days with the tall elevators at the Edinburgh and Imperial Dock and the Western Harbour making an impressive skyline.

Bus: 16
Open: There are no organized tours. To arrange a visit contact the Port Manager, Tower Place, Leith, Edinburgh EH6 7DB.
Tel: 031-554 4343/51

EXTRA . . . EXTRA . . . The port of Leith has become a meeting place for bird-watchers. Many rare seabirds and waders have been seen here including a Slavonian grebe and a little auk.

GLASS WORKS, 14–16 Holyrood Road

Although tiny, this studio and gallery is fascinating. You can stand back and enjoy the ancient art of glass-making and then browse around the exhibition of finished work. It's all exciting to watch but make sure you don't miss the part when the glass-maker gathers a ball of molten glass, still red-hot from the furnace, on to the end of a hollow iron tube and then skilfully blows, twists and turns the tube so that the glass takes shape. If the worker isn't too busy, he'll explain what he's doing and why.

Open: Tuesday–Saturday, 1000–1800

EXTRA . . . EXTRA . . . The main ingredient for glass-making is silica – extracted from sand on the coast of Argyll, opposite the Island of Mull.

LAWCOURTS, Parliament Square, off the Royal Mile

The queue which forms each morning waiting patiently for the doors to the public gallery to be opened, proves that the machinations of the law are as popular as ever. Not perhaps as blood-thirsty as the crowds which once gathered to watch a public execution, the people who are interested in murder trials and the like do have a somewhat macabre idea of what is entertaining. Nevertheless, the sight of the jury filing in, the barristers taking their seats, policemen on duty in doorways and the macer at work flitting about the courtroom *is* fascinating! One tip though – choose a seat neat the exit so that when you've seen all you want you can slip out easily.

Open: Monday–Friday, start 1000

EXTRA . . . EXTRA . . . 'Not proven' is a verdict you'll hear only in a Scottish court. It means that the case against the defendant has not been proved – that there is insufficient evidence to establish whether the accused person is guilty or innocent. The accused person is free to leave the court but is not free from the stigma of suspicion.

MARKET: EASTER ROAD, off Hawkhill Avenue

Well off the tourist track, this market is worth going to see if you're an overseas visitor and want to know how an ordinary market operates. The setting is a bleak car park, but you'll get a friendly welcome from stall-holders who can spot a new face a mile off! They sell ordinary, everyday household goods, fruit and vegetables. Not the place to hunt for souvenirs but you certainly won't meet other tourists!

Open: Sunday, 1000–1600

EXTRA . . . EXTRA . . . There are also sometimes markets in Newhaven and Chesser – but check with the Tourist Information Centre (Tel: 031-557 2727) for days and times. During the Festival (*see page 113*) there's often an extremely interesting market in Grassmarket (*see page 46*) but, once again, it's best to check details with the Tourist Information Centre.

MARKET: WAVERLEY MARKET, Princes Street

This is not so much a market, more a shopping precinct with a huge selection of stores, large and small, selling goods ranging from clothes and food to flowers. It was opened in 1984 and almost immediately became a hub of activity – in fact, people stand and watch the shoppers! The actual shopping area is indoors, making it a good spot to spend a few rainy hours. The roof, which is on street level, has been made into as pleasant a place as a 'concrete' park can be and there are plenty of benches and flowerbeds. It's also worth noting that Waverley Market is the home of the Tourist Information Centre (Tel: 031-557 2727).

Open: Shopping area: Monday–Saturday

Open area: all the time

EXTRA . . . EXTRA . . . A small but famous sweet shop used to stand on Waverley Steps. Renowned for Edinburgh Rock, it used to take sugar ration coupons in exchange for confectionery.

THE MUSEUM SHOP, 140 High Street, off the Royal Mile. Tel: 031-225 9566

Next door to the Edinburgh Wax Museum (fee), The Museum Shop is full of interesting bits and bobs . . . and the overpowering smell of candlewax. Downstairs, you can watch candles being dipped, shaped and decorated. It's a very simple process – in fact, although the idea of demonstrating candlemaking is obviously to tempt you to buy some of the weird and wonderful candles in the shop, you can't help feeling you could do it yourself at home!

Open: Monday–Saturday, 1000–1730

EXTRA . . . EXTRA . . . Candlemaker Row, at the top of George IV Bridge, is a steep and narrow street well worth wandering down. One of the 18th-century buildings in the street is Candlemaker Hall, built as a gathering point for the Incorporation of Candlemakers.

NEWSPAPER: THE SCOTSMAN, North Bridge. Tel: 031-225 2468

Down marble-clad corridors and stairs to see an old-fashioned typesetting machine – the excellent guided tour of *The Scotsman* starts quietly enough. Then on down more stairs towards a distant rumbling. The sound gets louder and louder; a door is opened and the most hellish noise bursts forth. Printing 45,000 newspapers an hour creates a deafening racket! Be prepared to yell your questions – but don't expect to be able to hear the reply. Overhead, endless streams of paper disappear in all directions. From seeming chaos, they reappear and fall into neat piles of freshly printed newspapers. If you're lucky you'll be given a free copy 'hot from the press'.

Open: by appointment only, *The Scotsman* makes visiting groups very welcome; to arrange a tour telephone then confirm in writing. Individuals (up to three people at a time) can join an organized party.

EXTRA . . . EXTRA . . . If you ask your guide he'll be delighted to tell you how Sean Connery once worked for *The Scotsman* and point out 007 locker!

POTTERY: ADAM POTTERY, 76 Henderson Row, Stockbridge. Tel: 031-557 3978

Stoneware is the most widely-used clay as it is very hard-wearing. Its hardness is achieved by firing at much higher temperatures than, say, for earthenware. If you want to watch the whole fascinating process and see a lump of clay expertly thrown on a potter's wheel, shaped, then fired in a kiln, go along to the Adam Pottery in Stockbridge (*see page 134*). This small, friendly pottery, which sells a whole range of domestic ware, makes visitors very welcome. There's also a terrarium workshop here – if you don't know what a terrarium is, go and take a look!

Bus: 34, 35
Open: Monday–Saturday, 1000–1700. (Remember these are places of work and it may not always be possible to watch the potter. Also, the workshops are very small so are unsuitable for large group visits.)

EXTRA . . . EXTRA . . . A number of unusual characters made from clay became associated with Scottish potteries. The two most well known are the 'Pirly Pig' (a piggy bank) and the 'Wally Dug' (a china dog).

SILVERSMITH: ADRIAN HOPE AND LINDA LEWIN WORKSHOP, 3a Henderson Place, Stockbridge. Tel: 031-556 6432

If you can afford to buy silver, it will probably be in the form of jewellery, but most modern jewellers have also trained as silversmiths and will jump at the chance of a commission in silverware. This is certainly true of Adrian Hope and Linda Lewin who together produce a wide range of items from bangles and earrings to ceremonial cups. You can visit their workshop in Stockbridge (*see page 134*) and watch them using traditional hand tools.

Bus: 34, 35
Open: By appointment only. Telephone or write well in advance.

EXTRA . . . EXTRA . . . It's interesting to think that the design of silverware has come full circle: during the

18th century silver goods were very simple in design; during the Victorian era they became highly decorative and elaborate; now, designers in silver have reverted once more to an elegant simple style.

CHAPTER FOUR

Museums, Galleries and Collections

ARTISTS' COLLECTIVE GALLERY, 52-4
High Street, off the Royal Mile.

Lack of money makes this small gallery a little stark. Anyone can exhibit their work here subject to it being passed by a selection committee – so a visit means taking pot luck! But if you *are* lucky you'll see something exciting and get a good idea of how contemporary young artists in Edinburgh see the world.

Open: Tuesday, Wednesday, Friday, 1230–1730; Thursday, 1230–1900; Saturday 1030–1700

EXTRA . . . EXTRA . . . Nearby Tweeddale Court contains the former mansion of the Marquises of Tweeddale. The building, dated 1576, later became the publishing house of Oliver and Boyd and at one time was the office of the British Linen Bank.

BRAIDWOOD AND RUSHBROOK FIRE MUSEUM, McDonald Road, off Leith Walk.
Tel: 031-228 2401

Don't be alarmed if your guide is called on duty halfway through your tour – the museum is attached to a working fire station and all the guides are firemen. The Edinburgh Fire Brigade, thought to be the oldest municipal fire brigade in the world, was set up in 1824 to help prevent the many fires which were sweeping through the built-up area of the city and causing havoc. The museum traces the history of the fire brigade through old uniforms, pictures and equipment, and brings you right up to date with a look inside a fire engine of today with all its various appliances.

Bus: 7, 10, 12, 16, 22, 25, 37, 49
Open: by appointment only

EXTRA . . . EXTRA . . . The first records of fire precautions in Scotland date from 1426 when town officers were informed that they should have 'seven or aught twenty fute ledders as well as three or foure sayes [saws] to the common use, and sex or ma cleikes of iron [long poles tipped with iron hooks] to draw down timbers and ruiffes that are fired'.

BRASS RUBBING CENTRE, Canongate Tolbooth, 163 Canongate, off the Royal Mile. Tel: 031-225 1131

There's a charge to make a rubbing, but it won't cost you a penny just to look – and there's certainly plenty to see. The centre contains a fascinating collection of brasses which have been moulded from medieval church brasses, Pictish stones and rare Scottish brasses. Look out for the beautiful Celtic Circle which is one of the most popular brasses in the centre. And don't miss the brass of Robert the Bruce, King of Scotland. The centre is extremely friendly and the assistant will be more than pleased to tell you about the origins of the brasses displayed.

Open: January–May, (Monday–Saturday), 1000–1645;
June–September, 1000–1800, Sunday, 1200–1745
(during the Festival only)

EXTRA . . . EXTRA . . . Robert the Bruce reigned over
Scotland from 1306 to 1329 during which time he managed
to negotiate a truce with England which lasted for thirteen
years.

CANONGATE TOLBOOTH, 163 Canongate, off the Royal Mile. Tel: 031-225 1131 ex 6638

Built in 1591 on the site of an earlier 'tolbuith', this is
one of the oldest surviving 16th-century buildings in
Canongate. It was originally a courthouse with cells below
but is now a city museum with permanent and temporary
exhibitions housed at the top of a wonderful winding
staircase. You can be sure to find something of interest
here – including the actual French-style building itself.
(*See Brass Rubbing Centre, page 86.*)

Open: Monday–Saturday, January–May 1000–1700;
June–September, 1000–1800

EXTRA . . . EXTRA . . . Canongate was once an inde-
pendent burgh. It was named after the Canons of the
Abbey of Holyrood.

CENTRAL LIBRARY, George IV Bridge. Tel: 031-225 5584

This is the main public library in Edinburgh and everyone
is free to use the reference facilities, so you can spend a

pleasant hour or so just browsing through the books. If you have a library ticket from any UK library then you can also borrow books for your stay. The Edinburgh Room is probably the most interesting feature. This is full of photographs, maps, newspaper cuttings, prints – all to do with Edinburgh past and present. If you're keen to know more about the history and making of Edinburgh, then take a copy of the free leaflet 'Books on Edinburgh'. This also has the addresses and telephone numbers of the other twenty-one branch libraries in Edinburgh.

Open: Monday–Friday, 0900–2030; Saturday, 0900–1300

EXTRA . . . EXTRA . . . This library is built on the site of a 17th-century mansion belonging to Sir Thomas Hope, King's Advocate to Charles I. Inside, you can still see remains of two original lintels above the doorways.

CITY ART CENTRE, 2–4 Market Street. Tel: 031-225 1131 ex 6380

Built in 1899, the City Art Centre was once a storehouse for *The Scotsman* (*see Newspaper page 80*) whose offices are next door. The building has also been used to store fruit and vegetables. But after an award-winning transformation in 1980, this Victorian warehouse became a popular art centre. Exhibitions held here are wide-ranging – from children's art to women's committee work in support of striking miners; from 'inspirational' photography to cloth wall-hangings. There's also an excellent permanent collection which is well worth taking a look at. It includes interesting paintings of Edinburgh during the 18th and 19th centuries – its people, buildings and street life – which will give you a good idea of how the city has grown and changed.

Open: January–May 1000–1700 June to September, Monday–Saturday, 1000–1800. During the Festival, Sundays, 1400–1700

EXTRA . . . EXTRA . . . There's a very useful flight of steps from North Bridge down to Market Street (they seem to go on for ever if you're walking up them!). During the Festival Fringe (*see page 113*) they're used as an informal gallery for local artists.

CLAN TARTAN CENTRE, James Pringle Woollen Mill, 70–74 Bangor Road, Leith. Tel: 031-553 5161/2

To reach this exhibition, set up in the far corner of the factory shop, you have to walk through rows upon rows of tartan kilts and accessories in an amazing range of colours – an education in itself! The exhibition takes the form of an audio-visual presentation which traces the history of tartan from the earliest records, dated 1538, when James V, father of Mary Queen of Scots, bought 'three ells of Heland Tartane', through 1747 and the Proscription Act which banned the wearing of tartan, to 1822 and the day George IV gave tartan the Royal seal of approval by appearing at the Palace of Holyroodhouse clad in a tartan kilt. The film does have a commercial slant, but if you try to forget they're encouraging you to buy, then you can learn a lot.

Incidentally, there's also an 'Archive Computer' which, given your name, will print out information about clan connections, war-cries, heraldic crests and so on – but you do have to pay for the service. However, the staff will explain for free how it all works and you'll come away with the sneaking suspicion that even though your name might not be MacDonald, Scottish blood runs through your veins!

Bus: 7, 22, 25, 34, 35
Open: Monday–Saturday, 0900–1730

EXTRA . . . EXTRA . . . During World War I, soldiers wearing their tartans were known by the Germans as the 'Ladies from Hell'.

FRUITMARKET GALLERY, 29 Market Street, Tel: 031-225 2383

This small gallery is housed on two floors. Simple and rather cold, it nevertheless provides a good setting for contemporary works of art. The lower space is particularly suitable for large sculptures of the sort which are hard to show to advantage in a more conventional gallery. The exhibitions in Fruitmarket Gallery change regularly and the friendly staff are often able to supply you with the details of the exhibiting artists' life and work.

Open: Monday–Saturday, 1000–1730

EXTRA . . . EXTRA . . . Another good reason to visit an exhibition here, any exhibition, is the excuse to sit in its café and eat scrumptious home-made cakes!

---

*SCOTTISH NATIONAL GALLERY OF MODERN ART, Belford Road. Tel: 031-556 8921

The actual building is almost as impressive as the gallery's contents, and that's no mean statement – this collection of modern art is said to be the most important in Britain outside the Tate Gallery in London. The 19th-century building with its portico of Doric columns was formerly John Watson's School and was converted to house the collection, formally opened in August 1984. The permanent exhibition which represents 20th-century artists in Europe and America, including Picasso, Hockney, Matisse and Giacometti, is found downstairs in twelve separate galleries. Temporary exhibitions are displayed upstairs. If you ever visited the gallery when it was in Inverleith Park you'll notice a huge difference. It's altogether better lit, better proportioned and a more pleasant place to muse. There's also a café serving light refreshments for foot-weary visitors.

Open: Monday–Saturday, 1000–1700; Sunday, 1400–1700 (open until 1800 during Festival)

EXTRA . . . EXTRA . . . The gallery is set in 12 acres of glorious parkland. With statues dotted about, views over the Pentland Hills (*see page 25*) and the Water of Leith it makes a lovely place for a summer stroll.

HM GENERAL REGISTER HOUSE, Princes Street. Tel: 031-556 6585

This sandstone building, designed by Robert Adam, is the headquarters of the Scottish Record Office and repository for Scotland's most important public records which fill 13 miles of shelving. Some records kept here date back to the 12th century. They include registers of the Great Seal (from 1315) and Privy Seal (from 1488), registers of the Court of Session and High Court of Justice and many other local authority, church and family

archives. You probably won't want to use the Historical
Search Room for studying purposes, but it's worth stepping inside to enjoy the quiet calm of the place and soak
up the atmosphere. Don't be put off by the fact that you
need to be issued with a reader's ticket; this is a mere
formality and you'll find the staff ready and willing to
explain the history and importance of the archives. The
Scottish Record Office also produces a series of free
leaflets, with details of the facilities open to the public,
which you can pick up at the reception. As you leave the
building, take a look at the statue of the Duke of
Wellington, erected in 1852, which stands at the front.
You should also visit West Register House (*see page
108*), another branch of the Scottish Record Office where
the more modern records are stored.

Open: Monday–Friday, 0900–1645

EXTRA . . . EXTRA . . . The clock on the North British
Hotel opposite West Register House has always been set
two minutes fast. This is to give passengers travelling
from the nearby Waverley Station a better chance of
catching their trains!

---

*HUNTLY HOUSE (City Museum), 142 Canongate, off the Royal Mile. Tel: 031-225 1131 ex 6689

There's a wealth of local history behind the doors of this
finely restored 16th-century timber-framed mansion. The
house, which gets its name from George, 1st Marquis of
Huntly, who was supposed to have lived here in 1636, is
now one of Edinburgh's principal museums. The exhibits
are varied, including collections of Edinburgh silver and
glass, Scottish pottery, relics related to Field-Marshal

Earl Haig (a World War I general), and a copy of the National Covenant signed in 1638 (*see Greyfriars Church, page 47*). However, it is the reconstructed room sets, such as the 1920s clay pipe workshop, which really paint the picture of local industry and domestic life.

Open: Monday–Saturday, 1000–1700; June to September, 1000–1800; Sunday (during the Festival only), 1400–1700

EXTRA . . . EXTRA . . . The Royal Mile was a precarious place to walk in the mid 18th century, the so-called 'Golden Age'. There was no drainage and citizens would fling all their rubbish and slops into the street below – and sometimes on to people's heads! The only warning given was the cry of 'gardy loo', a corruption of the French '*gare de l'eau*'.

JULES THORN HISTORICAL HALL
(Museum of the Royal College of Surgeons), 18 Nicholson Street. Tel: 031-556 6206

Until 1955, it was the tradition of the Royal College of Surgeons that all items in its collection should be on display. The result was an extremely overcrowded exhibition area. The collection displayed today, in the Jules Thorn Historical Hall, is both selective and extremely interesting. It covers the history of medicine and many of its important personalities. (*See also Menzies Campbell Collection, page 95; Pathology Collection, page 100.*)

Open: weekdays – telephone for times

EXTRA . . . EXTRA . . . In 1699, the Guild of Barber Surgeons of Edinburgh put an advertisement in the

Edinburgh Gazette announcing their intention to create a museum: 'these are to give notice that the Chirurgeon Apothecaries of Edinburgh are erecting a library of Physicall, Anatomicall, Chirurgicall, Botanicall Pharmaceuticall and other Curious books . . . They are also making a collection of all naturall and artificiall curiosities', and they invited 'any person [who] have such to bestow let them give notice'. Well the results almost 300 years later are impressive!

---

*LADY STAIR'S HOUSE, Lady Stair's Close, Lawnmarket. Tel: 031-225 1131 ex 6593

Tucked away in the corner of Lady Stair's Close (*see page 48*) is a small but fascinating museum devoted to Scotland's three most famous literary gentlemen – Robert Burns, Sir Walter Scott and Robert Louis Stevenson. It has a huge collection of manuscripts, paintings and relics, including the press used to print Sir Walter Scott's novels. The building itself is also of great interest and worth a visit in its own right. It was originally built in 1622 for Sir William Gray of Pittendrum, a merchant burgess of the city, and if you look at the door lintel you can still see the date and initials of Gray and his wife. Inside, it retains all its character and charm with a corner stair tower a special feature. (*See Robert Louis Stevenson Heritage Trail, page 58.*)

Open: Monday–Friday, 1000–1700 (June–September, 1000–1800)

EXTRA . . . EXTRA . . . Lady Stair's House takes its name from Elizabeth, the Dowager Countess of Stair, who lived here in the early 18th century. She was a leading light in the fashionable circles of high society and the inspiration for Sir Walter Scott's story *My Aunt Margaret's Mirror*.

MENZIES CAMPBELL COLLECTION (Museum of the Royal College of Surgeons), 18 Nicholson Street. Tel: 031-556 6206

If you don't like going to the dentist, don't visit this dental museum! But if you decide not to visit, you'll miss out on a really fascinating collection of dental instruments. True, they do look more like instruments of torture, but the decorative detail on some items is exquisite. Anyway, it certainly gives you something to think about the next time you have a filling. (*See also Jules Thorn Historical Hall, page 93; Pathology Collection, page 100.*)

Open: by appointment only

EXTRA . . . EXTRA . . . Dr J. Menzies Campbell donated his collection to the museum in 1965, even though he practised as a dentist in Glasgow.

MUSEUM OF LIGHTING (Mr Purves' Lighting Emporium), 59 Stephen Street. Tel: 031-556 4503

Chaotic, friendly, dusty, cluttered, intriguing – there are many ways to describe this unique museum. But perhaps the most apt of all is eccentric. A museum of lighting which is dimly lit? Yes, this is a very unusual place to visit. It's really a small private collection of gas, oil and electric lamps presided over by its enthusiastic owner.

There's a small shop which finances the museum – but don't be put off; its aim is to keep collectors' lamps working. If you show just a glimmer of interest in lighting you'll be made very welcome. You'll be told about a coach lamp used 100 years ago to help deliver a baby, shown a chimney collection (glass funnels for oil lamps) and, probably, be treated to a heated discussion on the politics of Scotland today. Think of a place totally unlike a museum – that's the Museum of Lighting!

Open: Saturday, 1100–1800 (or any time by appointment). This is a tiny museum, not the place for large groups.

EXTRA . . . EXTRA . . . If you're at all interested in lighting keep your eyes peeled when walking around Edinburgh; there are lots of old and unusual lamps to be spotted. And do save a bit of energy for a night walk (*see Walk 1 · Floodlit Edinburgh, page 139*) – it's worth the effort!

---

*NATIONAL GALLERY OF SCOTLAND, The Mound. Tel: 031-556 8921

This is a relatively small gallery by national gallery standards, certainly much smaller than, say, London's National Galley. However, that's a definite plus as it makes viewing the paintings a more manageable and enjoyable experience. Small it may be, but the quality of the collection is excellent. It includes masterpieces from every major period of western art. Make sure you see Raphael's 'Bridgewater Madonna!' 'Diana and Actaeon' by Titian; Rembrandt's 'Self Portrait'; and Van Gogh's 'Olive Trees'. There are also works by Monet, Degas, Gauguin, Renoir and Sisley. If you have only limited time to spend in the National Gallery, which is conveniently situated on The Mound (*see Festival Fringe, page 113*), collect a free gallery plan near the entrance; with it you will be able to plot a route which should include elements of all important artistic movements.

Open: Monday–Saturday, 1000–1700; Sunday, 1400–1700. Times vary during the Festival.

EXTRA . . . EXTRA . . . In the foyer of the National Gallery you can usually pick up a copy of *Art Work*, a free guide to arts and crafts in Edinburgh.

---

*NATIONAL LIBRARY OF SCOTLAND, George IV Bridge. Tel: 031-226 4531

This impressive building on George IV Bridge is one of the four largest libraries in Great Britain with a stock which includes many old and rare books. The collection was originally housed in the Advocate's Library, just behind Parliament Square, but was moved in 1925 to help found the National Library. Make sure you see the oldest book in the library (a copy of the Gutenberg Bible, printed in 1455), the last letter of Mary Queen of Scots, and the Chepman and Myllar prints, the first work printed in Scotland.

But there's a lot more going on at the National Library than shelves and displays of books and manuscripts; there's also an exhibition area and the library has a high reputation for excellent exhibitions on a wide range of topics. You'll find the staff extremely helpful and more than happy to explain all the library's facilities. You can also pick up free leaflets from the reception desk.

The Map Room is now at 137 Causeway (Tel: 031-667 7848). This claims to be the largest and most comprehensive map collection in the north of Britain and has over a million sheet maps and 10,000 atlases. Again, the staff will show you around, but you do have to sign the register of readers first.

Open: Reading Room: Monday 0930–1700; Tuesday–
                         Thursday, 0930–2030; Saturday
                         0930–1300

Exhibition: Monday–Friday,   0930–1700;
              Saturday 0930–1300
              Sunday (May–October), 1400–
              1700

Map Room: Monday–Friday,   0930–1700;
            Saturday, 0930–1300

EXTRA . . . EXTRA . . . The National Library is a copyright library which means that it is entitled to be sent a copy of every single work published in Great Britain.

---

*NATIONAL MUSEUM OF ANTIQUITIES OF SCOTLAND, Queen Street. Tel: 031-556 8921

This intriguing collection shouldn't be missed. It provides a comprehensive record of everyday Scottish life from the stone age to modern times. Remember Robinson Crusoe, the castaway who lived with Man Friday on a desert island? Well, the real-life Robinson Crusoe was a Scotsman named Alexander Selkirk. Find out lots more about this adventurer's unusual life in the museum's fascinating display. Look out, too, for the Maiden – a beheading machine which was made in Edinburgh in 1564 and used until 1710.

Open: Monday–Friday, 1000–1700; Sunday, 1400–1700
         Festival Monday–Saturday 1000–1800; Sunday
         1100–1800

EXTRA . . . EXTRA . . . Queen Street Gardens, which are beautiful, are privately owned and not open to the public. However, it's worth peering over the railings because the gardens are an intrinsic part of the designs for the New Town (*see Walk 4   New Town, page 151*).

NETHERBOW ARTS CENTRE, 43 High Street, off The Royal Mile. Tel: 031-556 2647

This arts centre, run by the Church of Scotland, stands beside John Knox's House – the home of the great reformer while he was minister at St Giles' (*see page 62*). The centre has three storeys: the top floor is where the major exhibitions are held, the first floor provides space for a reception area, shop and minor exhibitions, while the ground floor is taken over by an excellent café serving delicious home-baking. In the summer visitors can sit outside in the courtyard. It's not surprising that the Netherbow Arts Centre has become a favourite stopping place for Royal Mile (*see Walk 3, page 147*) walkers.

Open: Tuesday–Saturday, 1000–1600

EXTRA . . . EXTRA . . . The Netherbow Arts Centre is named after a gateway which used to be situated close by and marked the very edge of Edinburgh.

NEW TOWN CONSERVATION CENTRE, 13a Dundas Street. Tel: 031-556 7054

This is the place to visit to get the flavour – past, present and future – of the New Town of Edinburgh. This quarter of the town was the inspiration of a young architect, James Craig, whose plans won him the job of designing the New Town in 1766. Work started in 1767 and continued until 1833 shortly after the death of George IV when the city ran out of money. The New Town Conservation Committee, set up in 1970 to help preserve the New Town, has turned the centre into an exhibition area. There's also a reference library and a shop selling guides and posters. (*See also Walk 4   New Town, page 151.*)

Open: Monday–Friday, 0900–1300, 1400–1700

EXTRA . . . EXTRA . . . Craig was somewhat thwarted when it came to naming streets in the New Town. He planned to call what is now Princes Street, St Giles' Street but George III wouldn't hear of it. The king wanted it to be called Princes Street after the future George IV and Duke of York. The present Queen Street was originally called Forth Street, and Craig's Queen Street became Frederick Street.

PATHOLOGY COLLECTION (Museum of the Royal College of Surgeons), 18 Nicholson Street, Tel: 031-556 6206

Pickled and bottled, dissected and dated, the Pathology Collection is an unusual place to browse for an hour or two. The museum, although extremely helpful to genuine visitors, doesn't welcome people who come simply to ogle the pickled curiosities. So, unless pathology is your particular interest, it's perhaps best to keep to the Jules Thorn Historical Hall (*see page 93*) or the Menzies Campbell Collection (*see page 95*).

Open: by appointment only

EXTRA . . . EXTRA . . . The oldest item in the museum is a skeleton which has mummified muscles still attached to it.

PHILATELIC BUREAU, in the Post Office, Waterloo Place. Tel: 031-556 8661

A tiny but fascinating collection, well worth taking a look at when you're buying stamps for your postcards. It includes an interesting collection of British commemorative stamps such as Commonwealth Parliamentary Conference, National Nature Week, Shakespeare Festival, Robert Burns, Battle of Hastings and the Centenary of Lister's discovery of Antiseptic Surgery.

Open: Monday–Thursday, 0900–1630; Friday, 0900–1600

EXTRA . . . EXTRA . . . Displayed on the stairs which lead from the Post Office to the Philatelic Bureau are a musket, brace of pistols and side pouches carried by coach guards on the Edinburgh to London Mail Coach in the late 18th century.

PRIVATE GALLERIES

Dotted around Edinburgh are many small, private art galleries with changing exhibitions by different artists and on a variety of themes. Don't be afraid to walk in – you're perfectly welcome just to browse. Galleries worth a mention are the Richard Demarco Gallery, 10 Jeffrey Street (off The Royal Mile); The Torrance Gallery, 29b

Dundas Street; and the Malcolm Innes Gallery, 67 George Street. However, you'll find a full list of exhibitions around the city in *What's On in Edinburgh* – a diary of events available from hotels and the Tourist Information Centre (Tel: 031-557 2727).

EXTRA . . . EXTRA . . . For more about what's on in the way of exhibitions, concerts, dance and special 'arty' events in Edinburgh, it's worth calling at Inform, an arts information centre set up by The Scottish Arts Council at 19 Charlotte Square (Open: Monday–Thursday, 0900–1730; Friday, 0900–1700).

---

*ROYAL SCOTTISH MUSEUM, Chambers Street. Tel: 031-225 7534

Stuffed animals, which stare stiffly and rather sadly from glass cases, are always popular with children. The Royal Scottish Museum is full of them – animals and children! Particularly spectacular is the skeleton of a whale suspended from the ceiling, its ribbed shape dramatically echoing the iron girders of the gallery. The building is characteristically Victorian in its cast-iron construction, plate-glass and terracotta work. Its designer, Captain Francis Fowke (1823–65), was clearly influenced by Sir Joseph Paxton's Crystal Palace. The most spectacular exhibition space in the museum is the main hall: under a beautiful glass roof, surrounded by fountains and Asiatic art, palms and other greenery thrive. In other galleries there are displays of early fossils, sparkling minerals and colourful uniforms. Perhaps most interesting of all is the section showing the history of science and technology – look out for the giant waterwheel.

Open: Monday–Saturday, 1000–1700; Sunday, 1400–1700

EXTRA . . . EXTRA . . . Look out for the sculpted heads of Queen Victoria, Prince Albert, James Watt, Charles Darwin, Michelangelo and Sir Isaac Newton – you'll find them above doorways.

SCOTTISH AGRICULTURAL MUSEUM,
Royal Highland Showground, Ingliston. Tel: 031-333 2674

Set in the grounds of the Royal Highland Show, this museum really comes into its own during the four days of the show in June. However, it's open to visitors throughout the summer and although Ingliston is a little way out of Edinburgh, it's easily accessible by bus and you won't be disappointed when you get there. The collection, which includes room sets, life-sized models, tools, clothes, pictures, prints and an audio-visual display, gives a real insight into how past generations lived and worked in the different regions of rural Scotland. Scratching a living from the land was pretty hard work in those days – long hours and back-breaking tasks for poor pay. Just looking will probably leave you exhausted, so take time to collect your thoughts over a cup of tea in the cafe before heading back.

Bus: 16, 17, 38, 203, 204
Open: May–September, Monday–Friday, 1000–1600; Sunday, first Sunday of the month, 1200–1700

EXTRA . . . EXTRA . . . Don't miss the Arnold Foster-mother Piglet Feeder – every mother should have one!

SCOTTISH GALLERY, 94 George Street. Tel: 031-225 5955

From the outside this gallery looks rather like a fine art shop with artists' materials and postcards for sale, but a step inside will fill every contemporary art connoisseur's heart with pleasure. The gallery dislikes labelling but suggests that its range of paintings and prints covers 'a wide area from figurative and representational to abstraction and the avant-garde'. These works of art are for sale or hire, but there's nothing to stop you browsing. The gallery also organizes twenty-four exhibitions a year so it's worth asking for the dates.

Open: Monday–Saturday, 0900–1700

EXTRA . . . EXTRA . . . Sir John Sinclair lived at 133 George Street. He is best known as the compiler of the First Statistical Account of Scotland, the forerunner to the census, from 1815 to 1835. A tall man himself, he had fifteen children, all over six feet tall and the area in front of the house became known as 'Giants' Causeway'.

SCOTTISH NATIONAL PORTRAIT GALLERY, Queen Street. Tel: 031-556 8921

This is the place to visit if you need to brush up on your knowledge of Scotland's kings and queens. Many other famous men and women – Flora Macdonald, Robert Burns, David Hume, Sir Walter Scott – stare down from their frames. The varied collection includes work by Reynolds, Raeburn and Gainsborough. It is an interesting illustrated recording of the history of Scotland – its people, their activities and achievements. The reference section is also impressive, containing over 20,000 engraved portraits and a large collection of photographs.

Open: Monday–Friday, 1000–1700; Sunday 1400–1700 (extended opening times during the Festival)

EXTRA . . . EXTRA . . . When you're in Queen Street visiting the Portrait Gallery, take a look at no. 8, designed by Robert Adam in 1771.

SCOTTISH POETRY LIBRARY, Tweeddale Court, 14 High Street, off the Royal Mile. Tel: 031-557 2876.

If you're interested in poetry, this is just the place to browse for a few hours. The library, which was opened in 1982, aims to give Scottish poetry a well-deserved boost and the friendly staff are so enthusiastic you'll find yourself sharing their love of the Scottish poets. Most of the books are by modern and living poets but there are some from other periods too. The library organizes Poetry Readings throughout the year and will lend books and tapes.

Open: Tuesday and Wednesday, 1130–1400, 1530–2100
Thursday, 1400–2100
Friday and Saturday, 1130–1800
Sunday, 1400–1600

EXTRA . . . EXTRA . . . The 18th-century poet Allan Ramsay (*see Ramsay Lane, page 57*) was a great Scottish patriot, especially when it came to his favourite subject – poetry. He greatly admired 'these good old Bards' and wrote of them, 'Their poetry is the Product of their own

Country, not pilfered and spoiled in the Transportation from abroad: Their Images are native, and their Landskips domestick; copied from Fields and Meadows we every Day behold.'

STILLS (The Scottish Photography Group Gallery), 105 High Street, off the Royal Mile. Tel: 031-557 1140

Although housed in a period building on the Royal Mile (*see Walk 3, page 147*), Stills gallery is very modern. The plain white walls provide a perfect backdrop for its excellent photography exhibitions. They have included Paul Strand's Hebridean work; early French photographs; and recent American photography. Definitely a gallery well worth visiting – even if you're only at the snap-shot stage!

Open: times vary and the gallery closes between exhibitions – telephone for details

EXTRA . . . EXTRA . . . Not far away is Moubray House. From here the *Edinburgh Courant* was published, edited in 1710 by Daniel Defoe.

*TALBOT RICE ART CENTRE, University of Edinburgh, South Bridge. Tel: 031-667 1011 ex 4308

The long, long climb up spiral staircases is well worth the effort. At the top of all those steps awaits a superb collection of paintings hung on elegant walls, and a good selection of modern art. The main gallery, known as the Georgian Gallery, designed by William Playfair (*see also Upper Library Hall page 67*), is home for the University of Edinburgh's Torrie Collection of 16th- and 17th-century paintings. The calm, elegant atmosphere, comfortable chairs and magazines encourage you to relax and linger – it really is an exquisite way to savour both the important paintings and their beautiful surroundings. If you can summon up just a little extra energy, more spiral staircases from the Georgian Gallery lead to a high-level corridor. From here there's a fantastic view of the gallery and a chance to take a good look at the intricate decorative work and the exquisite detail. The second gallery of the Talbot Rice Art Centre is in complete contrast: designed to take changing exhibitions of contemporary art, it's light, airy and rather plain!

Open: Monday–Friday, 1000–1700; Saturday for special exhibitions.
During the Edinburgh Festival the times vary, telephone for details.

EXTRA . . . EXTRA . . . David Talbot Rice was professor of Fine Art at Edinburgh University from 1934 until his death in 1972, it was his idea to create the Art Centre.

TRADITIONAL PHARMACY, Pharmaceutical Society of Great Britain (Scottish Department), 36 York Place. Tel: 031-556 4386

There's nothing to guide you to this amazing exhibition housed in the lower floor of the Scottish headquarters of the Pharmaceutical Society. In fact, very few tourists even know it exists so you are almost guaranteed a personal guided tour. The room is set up as an exact replica of a pharmacist's shop of the late Victorian period. All the fittings are original – donated by Charles Drummond when he closed his shop in Grassmarket in 1960. They still hold bottles and jars filled with all sorts of weird and wonderful lotions and potions. Other exhibits have been given by interested pharmacists and members of the public. Everything's here – from a wooden powder measure to a set of weighing scales, a baby's glass feeding-bottle and a sachet of special cleaning agent for straw hats! As the guide explains, this is not a museum – you can touch all the exhibits and poke your nose into all the drawers and cupboards.

Open: Monday–Friday, 0900–1300,1400–1700

EXTRA . . . EXTRA . . . Look out for the blue jar for storing live leeches. These were used for sucking blood from patients as a way of purging them of illness. The society has been known to put on displays of live leeches!

WEST REGISTER HOUSE, Charlotte Square. Tel: 031-556 6585

A branch of the Scottish Record Office (*see also HM Register House, page 91*), this is where the records of modern government departments, the Scottish railways and nationalized industries are stored. There is also a collection of maps, plans and micofilms. The building was originally St George's Church, built in 1814 but closed for worship in 1961 due to dry rot and structural faults. It was converted and opened as West Register House in 1971. Although space in the Search Room is limited, any one is welcome to look at the exhibition of historical documents and portraits in the front hall. This display relates the making of Scotland as it is today.

Open: Search Room: Monday–Friday, 0900–1645
Exhibiton: Monday–Friday, 1000–1600

EXTRA . . . EXTRA . . . The archives were originally kept in Edinburgh Castle but in the 17th century they were moved to the Laigh (Low) Parliament House in the High Street where the papers proved a temptation for resident vermin and the clerks had to petition for a cat to keep the mice under control!

CHAPTER FIVE
Events and Entertainment

*BEATING THE RETREAT, Castle Espanade, Castle Rock

The esplanade to Edinburgh Castle (*see page 42*) is the floodlit setting for the famous Military Tattoo (fee) held during the Edinburgh Festival. However, it's also where the equally splendid, but free-to-watch, ceremony of Beating the Retreat takes place. Held during May and early June on two afternoons a week, it's a feast of colour and music. The sound of the massed pipe bands carries down the length of the Royal Mile (*see page 147*) and you're guaranteed plenty of traditional kilt swinging and tartan swirling!

Date: May and early June. For details contact the Tourist Information Centre (Tel: 031-557 2727).

EXTRA . . . EXTRA . . . June is also the month when the Queen traditionally pays a visit to Edinburgh. As you can imagine, the streets are lined with well-wishers and the pipe bands are out in full force.

---

*EDINBURGH FESTIVAL FRINGE

The Edinburgh Festival Fringe is known throughout the world and is now the largest arts festival of its kind anywhere. It started spontaneously in 1947 as an addition to the established Edinburgh International Festival and has since grown and grown. There's now a Fringe Society which offers performers and public help, advice and information. The Fringe operates in the belief that anyone with determination can put on, or be part of, a show; all who take part do their own thing at their own risk. The result is electrifying! The city buzzes and hums with activity, energy, colour and life. For three weeks during the summer every possible corner becomes a venue which explodes with fun and creativity. Large halls and the tops of letter boxes, playgrounds and parks, all become part of the Festival. Every single visitor is involved in its huge audience. You simply can't miss the Fringe!

There's free entertainment just about everywhere during the Festival Fringe, but some venues can be counted on for particularly good performances.

Wireworks Playground, behind Festival Fringe office, 170 High Street
Booked by the hour and in advance, this open space behind the Fringe office has some of the best free theatre, dance and music events of the festival. As each company is given only an hour, many now frequently organize their shows specifically to be performed in Wireworks Playground. Events start on the hour every hour, 1000–1700.

Parliament Square, off High Street
The events happening every thirty minutes in Parliament Square are less formalized than those performed in Wireworks – but sometimes more spectacular. One year the Japanese theatre company, Sankai Juku, dangled upside down from the Lothian Regional Council Building. They made a slow and very dramatic descent watched by huge crowds. The square is a favourite venue of the Smallest Travelling Theatre in the World – there's room for an

audience of only one! Most exciting of all is the Busking Competition which attracts dozens of unusual acts. But whenever you pass through Parliament Square, and as it's on the Royal Mile (*see Walk 3, page 147*) it's hard to miss, you can be sure of catching some impromptu event or colourful pageant.

The Mound, off Princes Street
During the Festival Fringe a visit to the Mound will make your head spin! It overflows with both performers and public as at least four events happen simultaneously. Also competing for attention are energetic individuals who show their skills – juggling, fire-eating, magic shows – on every possible scrap of space. If you're lucky you'll catch sight of the piping Reverend – just one of the regular 'characters' of the Festival. The Mound doesn't only attract street theatre; it's also popular with street artists. Imagine a 15 foot Mona Lisa, skilfuly drawn on the pavement with coloured chalks – it gets washed away with the first rains! There's a chance to buy a more permanent reminder of your visit to the Festival Fringe from one of the artists who display their work along the railings, or to have your portrait drawn by one of the many artists who set up their easels in the sunshine.

Wireworks, Parliament Square and The Mound are the main outdoor venues which shouldn't and really can't, be missed. There are also two main events which are well worth seeing – the Opening Cavalcade and Fringe Sunday.

The Opening Cavalcade of about forty floats, marching bands and vintage cars starts at Regent's Terrace, goes down Princes Street, up Lothian Road, down King's Stables and ends in Grassmarket (*see page 46*). It takes place on the first Sunday of Festival Fringe, 1430–1600.

Fringe Sunday used to be an incredibly crowded happening which took over the whole length of the Royal Mile
(*see page 147*). Just about everyone involved in the
Festival Fringe tried to cram into this one street and
display their skills. The crush became so dangerous that
Fringe Sunday was forced to move venue to Holyrood
Park (*see page 21*) where it's become known as 'a lark in
the park'. If the weather's good the event becomes a
huge picnic to which everyone is invited. Entertained by
Fringe groups who perform for free on five large lorries,
it's a great day out. The Festival Fringe office also
commissions events which have included a dancing bear
and man-lifting kites. It takes place on the second Sunday
of Festival Fringe, 1200–1600.

Further information from:	The Festival Fringe Society; 170 High Street, Edinburgh EHI IQS. Tel: 031-226 5257/9. Open Monday-–Saturday, 1000–1800; Sunday 1130–1800 (telephones open until 1900 during the Festival for information and booking).

EXTRA . . . EXTRA . . . The Edinburgh International
Festival includes opera, ballet, classical music, theatre,
exhibitions and the world famous Military Tattoo. Most
of the events are not free but there are often displays in
the venue foyers which are worth going to look at; check
with the Tourist Information Centre (Tel: 031-557 2727)
for details.

EDINBURGH FOLK FESTIVAL

Folk comes to Edinburgh in a big way during the week-
long annual folk festival, and many of the events are

free. It's folk in its widest sense – one year saw a day of Indian music and culture including a show of Indian cookery, with a chance to try your hand at making chapatis, and demonstrations of traditional Indian printing. All sorts of bands, dance troupes and craftspeople come to the different venues in Edinburgh – putting on concerts, dance workshops, demonstrations, competitions, puppet shows, lectures and exhibitions and setting up craft stalls. So even if you're not keen on folk music, you'll find something of interest during the week.

Date: March/April
Further information from: Edinburgh Folk Festival, Shillinghill, Temple, Midlothian EH23 4SH *or* Tourist Information Centre (Tel: 031-557 2727); *or* (during the Folk Festival) The Festival Club, Teviot Row House, Teviot Row. Tel: 031-667 2091, open: 0900–1500

EXTRA . . . EXTRA . . . Look out for the annual competition staged by a group of people who call themselves 'Lunatic Fringe'. They specialize in running extraordinary events at folk festivals and past events have included a solo spoons-laying contest and one-man-band championship.

---

*FIREWORKS, Castle Esplanade

Every year thousands of people gather in Princes Street Gardens (*see page 26*) to watch the display of fireworks set off from the Castle esplanade. The show is spectacular with shimmering cascades of 'Star Shells', avalanches of

'Sparkling Snow' and of course lots of 'Roman Candles'. It's part of the annual Festival of Fireworks Concert which was first performed in 1950 when Sir Thomas Beecham conducted Handel's 'Music for the Royal Fireworks'. He must have looked an unusual sight dressed in traditional tails but with a steel helmet on his head to protect him from sparks!

Date: varies – ask at the Tourist Information Centre (Tel: 031-557 2727) for details

---

EXTRA . . . EXTRA . . . There are firework displays throughout Edinburgh on 5 November to celebrate Guy Fawkes night. Some of them are free; ask at the Tourist Information Centre for details of times and venues.

GENERAL ASSEMBLY OF THE CHURCH OF SCOTLAND, Assembly Hall, The Mound

Each year in May, ministers from all over Scotland come to Edinburgh for a week of decision-making and debate over future policies of the Church of Scotland. The assembly is chaired by the Moderator of the Church of Scotland, the highest office in the Church. Although members of the public can't watch the meeting take place, crowds line the streets to enjoy the spectacle as ministers march, to the sound of pipes and drums, from the Palace of Holyroodhouse (*see page 54*) to the Assembly Hall. If the Queen is staying at the palace, she attends. If not she sends her Lord High Commissioner.

Date: for details contact the Tourist Information Centre (Tel: 031-557 2727)

EXTRA . . . EXTRA . . . The first 'General Assemblie of this haill Realme' dates back to 1560, and the tradition of the ruling monarch being present has been held since then. It was only broken by Mary Queen of Scots who, as a Roman Catholic, refused to recognize the Church of Scotland.

HOGMANAY

Hogmanay is now well known as a uniquely Scottish way of welcoming in the New Year. However, the notion of dancing, drinking and singing 'Auld Lang Syne' is relatively new, dating from the late 18th century. In 1790 it was noted that 'on the last night of the year visitors and company made a point of not separating until after the clock had struck twelve, when they rose, and, mutually kissing, wished each other a happy New Year'. You can sample the fun of this now traditional midnight custom by joining the crowds who gather to hear the bells of the now closed-down Tron Church in the High Street strike twelve. On the last note the street celebrations of Hogmanay begin!

Date: 31 December
Time: 2400

EXTRA . . . EXTRA . . . The origin of the word Hogmanay isn't very clear. But in his *Dictionary of the Scottish Language* Jamieson defines it as 'The name appropriated by the vulgar to the last day of the year'!

JAZZ PARADE, Regent Road to Princes Street

If jazz is your interest don't miss this colourful parade; but even if you're not a fan it's still worth going. The

parade is a prelude to the week long Festival of Jazz.
Thousands of people gather along its route to watch and
hundreds take part walking alongside the companies of
marching bands, majorettes and vintage cars. It's certainly
noisy and lots of fun!

Date: August. Contact the Tourist Information Centre
for full details (Tel: 031-557 2727)

EXTRA . . . EXTRA . . . Maybe it's the influence of
Edinburgh's student population but a large number of
the city's pubs offer free entertainment. Well, you have
to buy at least a fruit juice but it's worth it for free
theatre, games, music and comic shows. Ask the Tourist
Information Centre (Tel: 031-557 2727) for details.

MAY DAY, Arthur's Seat

May Day is a magical day in Edinburgh, and a super-
stitious one too. According to folklore, you can have a
wish at St Anthony's Well near Arthur's Seat (*see page
13*). Although the well is now enclosed, it's still fun to
make your way across the fields and hope your wish
comes true. Why not follow the age-old custom of washing
your face in the May Day dew while you're there? This is
supposed to bring you good luck for the coming year and
make your complexion clear and beautiful. Whether you
believe it or not, it's still a charming tradition!

Date: 1 May

EXTRA . . . EXTRA . . . The Act of Union between
England and Scotland was passed on 1 May 1707. There's
a story that on the same day someone sneaked into the

tower of St Giles' Cathedral (*see page 62*) and played an old Scottish tune on the bells – 'How can I be sad on my wedding day?'

*OPEN AIR DANCING, Princes Street Gardens

With lots of nifty footwork and arm waving, the sight of dancers leaping to the steps of the Highland Fling certainly puts a spring in your step and makes you feel like joining in. Dancing sessions, to old-time music and traditional Scottish tunes, are held four times a week during the summer months from June to September, in Princes Street Gardens. (*See also Park Band Concerts, below*).

Time: for more information contact the Tourist Information Centre (Tel: 031-557 2727)

EXTRA . . . EXTRA . . . A favourite Scottish dance is 'The Dashing White Sergeant' which is based on Pas de Basque and reel steps. This traditional country dance has also been adapted to ballroom style.

PARK BAND CONCERTS, Princes Street Gardens

Take your sandwiches along to Princes Street Gardens (*see page 26*) during the summer months from June to September and you'll be able to munch your lunch to the sound of music. There's a full and changing programme of rousing music with bands dressed in colourful costume meeting to play from the Ross Bandstand. It's no wonder the gardens have become a favourite picnic place for office workers and visitors. (*See also Open Air Dancing, page 121.*)

Time: for details contact the Tourist Information Centre (Tel: 031-557 2727)

EXTRA . . . EXTRA . . . Listen out for the loud boom of the 'One O'Clock' gun as a time-ball drops from the top of the Nelson Monument (*see page 52*) and startles unsuspecting tourists. This used to be a clock-check used mainly by Leith mariners.

WELSH CORNER BI-CENTENNIAL EVENT, Usher Hall, Lothian Road

Every other year the thistles of Scotland compete with the leeks of Wales as rugby supporters get together to watch the annual Wales v Scotland Rugby International held on alternate years at Murrayfield. After the game, there's a free concert in Usher Hall. The voices are always harmonious and the evening enjoyable whichever team has won the match!

Date: March. For details contact the Tourist Information Centre (Tel: 031-557 2727)

EXTRA . . . EXTRA . . . Usher Hall is the main concert hall in Edinburgh. It was built in Renaissance style in 1914 with a grant of £100,000 from Andrew Usher, distiller and leading whisky blender. Incidentally, the clock outside was a gift from another distiller, Arthur Bell.

CHAPTER SIX

Villages in and around Edinburgh

COLINTON, 5½ miles (9km) west of Edinburgh

Colinton is both a pretty and a wealthy village, situated beside the Water of Leith, which was once used to power watermills. There was also a distillery and a skinnery here which, along with agriculture, provided ample employment. In 1875 Colinton was linked to Edinburgh by railway and it quickly became popular with wealthy commuters who built large houses (*see Spylaw Park, page 29*). The railway is now a pleasant walk linking Colinton with Slateford (*see page 28*) but you can see the station master's cottage in Spylaw Bank Road, linked to the platform of the former station by a flight of wooden steps known as 'Jacob's Ladder'. As you wander round the village, look out for the parish church (*see Colinton Church, page 40*) and Old Boag's Mill which in 1735 made paper for bank notes.

Bus: 16

EXTRA . . . EXTRA . . . There's an old yew tree in the manse (vicarage) garden which was mentioned by Robert Stevenson in *Kidnapped*.

CORSTORPHINE, 4½ miles (7km) west of Edinburgh

Corstorphine can no longer rightly be called a village; old paintings depict cottages and open fields, but today the picture is very different. Clearly a suburb of Edinburgh, Corstorphine has developed quickly during this century and is now filled with shops and office blocks. Remnants of old Corstorphine have survived, notably its church (*see page 40*) and an impressive ancient, stone dovecot which is all that remains of the estate of Corstorphine Castle. The dovecote is large, circular and contains 1,060 nests, at one time providing fresh food for the laird and fertilizer for his crops.

Bus: 12, 26, 31

EXTRA . . . EXTRA . . . Near the dovecote is a large old sycamore tree – its girth is 12 feet and its height some 55 feet (17m). Beneath its branches, James Lord Forester was stabbed by his lover Christian Nimmo in 1679 – locals will tell you how her unhappy ghost haunts it.

---

*CRAMOND, 7 miles (11km) north of Edinburgh

Cramond is a beautiful spot situated at the mouth of the river Almond, where it forms a perfect natural harbour. The Romans, in A.D. 140, built a fort here which they occupied for seventy years (*see Roman Fort, page 59*). Now Cramond is little more than a few white-washed workers' cottages huddling together beside a yacht-filled harbour. Picturesque it certainly is, and there's more to see and do than would at first appear. Thankfully, Cramond isn't spoiled by rows of gift shops, but it's very popular and best avoided at the weekend as its few small streets can become extremely congested. Visitors come to see the exhibition at The Maltings or to have a lunchtime drink at the Inn. The real delight of Cramond,

however, is the wild bird life and the walking. On a walk
along the seafront at low tide you should be able to spot
a large number of waders; redshanks and knots are
common and oystercatchers also enjoy feeding on the
wet sands; there are plenty of gulls and you might glimpse
a curlew or an Arctic tern. All in all it's busy down on
the seafront when the tide's out!

Other things to look out for are: a medieval tower and
Cramond Church with its well-kept, walled churchyard.
When you've seen all you want to see in Cramond, take a
walk along the wide waterside espanade which, if you're
feeling energetic, will take you all the way to Granton.

Bus: 4, 9, 10

EXTRA . . . EXTRA . . . Along with wading birds at
low tide there are wading humans – digging for bait!

---

*DEAN VILLAGE, 1½ miles (2½km) from Princes Street

A pretty way to reach this pristine little village is along a
pathway which begins at Balford Bridge.

Set in a valley, and sheltered by steep wooded slopes,
it is in a perfect position. Indeed, there has been a
settlement here for 800 years. The Water of Leith, which
flows through Dean, was early in the village's history
harnessed to provide power for milling. At one time this
small river powered some seventy mills from Forth to
Pentlands; most have now disappeared. Today Dean is
being promoted as a tourist attraction – not as somewhere
to stay, but as a place to catch a glimpse of traditional
domestic Scottish architecture. Buildings have been given
new lives – stables and coach houses turned into offices,

others restored to provide homes. Look out for the baker's sign, a symbolic wheatsheaf, on the wall of Bell's Brae House.

Bus: 18, 20, 41

EXTRA . . . EXTRA . . . When standing on Dean Bridge, designed in 1832 by Thomas Telford, don't be deceived by the church you can see – it's an electricity sub-station!

DUDDINGSTON, 2½ miles (4km) south of Princes Street

This tiny village nestles on the edge of Duddingston Loch, while behind it looms Arthur's Seat (*see page 13*). It's a pretty spot, secluded from the rest of Edinburgh's sprawling development by the expanse of Holyrood Park (*see page 21*) and it retains a sense of village intimacy. As with most small villages, the most prominent building is the church (*see page 41*) but there's also an interesting building where Bonnie Prince Charlie is said to have stayed before the Battle of Prestonpans – ask a local to point it out to you. Most visitors go to Duddingston either to play golf or to do some bird-watching as Duddingston Loch is now a bird sanctuary.

Bus: 21, 36, 422 to Holyrood Park

EXTRA . . . EXTRA . . . The Sheeps Head Inn is said to be the oldest licensed premises in Scotland – look out for its skittle alley.

GRANTON, 4 miles (6½km) north of Edinburgh

Granton isn't a picturesque spot to visit, dominated as it is by a huge gas container. However, it's popular with golfers as there's an extensive course alongside the river Forth. But the best reason to visit Granton is to start a seafront walk to the very pretty ancient Roman settlement of Cramond (*see page 126*).

Bus: 8, 9, 10, 16, 22

EXTRA . . . EXTRA . . . Though catering for yachts, Granton's harbour is still a place of work. It was constructed in 1835 and a steam ferry which operated from here to Burntisland was the regular means of transport between Edinburgh and Fife before the Forth Bridge was built.

INVERESK, 7½ miles (12km) east of Edinburgh

Inveresk is very near Musselburgh (*see page 130*) but it's somehow both shielded from it and protected by it. The village is exceptionally attractive and has been used by numerous film crews for period settings. When you wander through its quiet streets you can easily see why. Huddled in a fairly bleak farmland setting, Inveresk is full of stone walls and closed doors. The buildings seem idealized and in some way secret. Peep over the walls and peer through gates – you won't be disappointed. The village church, St Michael's (*see page 65*), is worth visiting. From here there are excellent views across roof-tops to the Firth of Forth and the sea. A small lane opposite the church leads down to the river – a pleasant spot to stop for a picnic.

Bus: 131

EXTRA . . . EXTRA . . . Inveresk Lodge and gardens
are now the property of the National Trust of Scotland
(fee). During the floods of 1948 its 4 acres of formal rose
gardens were washed away in just one night.

KIRKLISTON, 10½ miles (17km) west of Edinburgh

If you're visiting South Queensferry (*see page 133*), then
take a look at the village of Kirkliston just 2 miles away.
As its name implies, the main feature is the Norman
church. This was built around 1200 and dedicated
(although it's not known to which saint) in 1244. Much of
the original still remains, but the church is noted for the
impressive romanesque south doorway, built in 1822.
While you're in the village, walk along to Castle House,
25 High Street, which is dated 1682 and is inscribed with
the initials of the owner and his wife.

Bus: 38

EXTRA . . . EXTRA . . . Niddrie Castle, now partially
in ruins, stands just a few miles away. This was where
Mary Queen of Scots stayed on her first night after
escaping from Loch Leven Castle in 1568.

MUSSELBURGH, 7½ miles (12km) east of Edinburgh

Some five miles east of Edinburgh's centre, Musselburgh
can be seen on a clear day from the top of Calton Hill

(*see page 17*). Situated on the coast its bay was once a haven for small fishing boats. Now Musselburgh is known primarily for its seafront race course – one of the smallest in the United Kingdom. There's also a popular golf course. The village itself has mainly 17th- and 18th-century houses and several pretty churches. Look out for St Andrew's church with its *very* tidy gardens.

Bus: 106, 107, 124, 125, 129

EXTRA . . . EXTRA . . . Fishwives from Musselburgh sold oysters, mussels and fish in Edinburgh around the St Giles' (*see page 62*) area. They called out their wares as they walked the streets with heavy creels on their backs. Lady Nairne, hearing their calls, made popular the song:

> Wha'll buy my caller herrin'?
> They're bonny fish an' halesome farin'
> Wha'll buy my caller herrin'
> New drawn frae the Forth?

> Wha'll buy my caller herrin'
> O ye may ca' them vular ferin'
> Wives an' mithers maist desparin'
> Ca' them lives o'men.

NEWHAVEN, 4 miles (6½km) north of Edinburgh

This picturesque village has been a port since the beginning of the 16th century when James IV decided to build a Scottish navy. As the water at Leith (*see Docks, page 75*) was too shallow to build his flagship *Great Michael*, new docks were built – 'Novus Portus de Leith' (Newhaven). But Newhaven soon flourished not as a dockyard but as a fishing port. The fishermen's cottages have now been restored — take a look at Fishmarket Square and Lamb's Court — but they lack the bustling charm of less completely preserved buildings. The harbour is pretty and small fishing boats still moor here. It's possible, on a damp blustery day, to imagine the old fishwives in their colourful costumes loading their baskets with fish to sell, with shouts of 'Caller Ou!', in the streets of Edinburgh.

Bus: 7, 11

EXTRA . . . EXTRA . . . Scottish tradition has it that no fishing boat should sail before midnight on a Sunday or it will be lost at sea.

PORTOBELLO, 4 miles (6½km) east of Edinburgh

Situated about three miles east of Princes Street, Portobello is Edinburgh's mini Blackpool. It has a mile-long sandy beach flanked by a popular promenade. One-armed bandits, ice-cream vendors and amusements make it a fun place for children, while parents can sit and take in the views across the Forth to Fife. The shipping channel is always full of activity as tankers, cargo and fishing boats make their way out to sea or into the busy port of Leith (*see Docks, page 75*).

Bus: 26

EXTRA . . . EXTRA . . . Sir Harry Lauder was born at 3 Bridge Street, Portobello, in 1870.

ROSLIN (ROSSLYN), 9 miles (14½km) south of Edinburgh

Most visitors to Roslin come to see the famous chapel founded in 1446 by William St Clair, Earl of Orkney and Roslin, and renowned for its elaborate carvings. There's an admission charge to go inside, but you can get a good view just walking round the outside. Next to the chapel is the site of the Old Rosslyn Inn (1660–1866) which entertained many notable people including King Edward VII as Prince of Wales, Dr Samuel Johnson, the Wordsworths and James Boswell. Looming above is the ancient Roslin Castle, once a moated stronghold much written about by Sir Walter Scott.

Wandering through the village, you get beautiful views of the Pentland Hills (*see page 25*) and it's pleasant to recall the days when the whole area was a forest.

Bus: 17

EXTRA . . . EXTRA . . . The name of the village derives from two Celtic words – *ross*, a rocky promontory, and *lynn*, a waterfall.

---

*SOUTH QUEENSFERRY, 4½ miles (15km) west of Edinburgh

Nestling between the two Forth Bridges (*see page 19*), on the south side of the Firth of Forth, is the beautiful village of South Queensferry, which until 1964 and the opening of the Forth Road Bridge was important as a ferry point. The Queensferry, which dates back at least 800 years, was named after Queen Margaret who used the ferry to cross from Edinburgh Castle to her palace at

Dunfermline in the 11th century. Today, the village is noted as a marvellous viewpoint for the two bridges and there are plenty of seats so you can sit and enjoy the views. However, you'll find a walk around the village, which is full of historic interest, just as pleasurable. There are lots of inviting passageways and steps to explore.

Attractions not to be missed include the Priory Church of St Mary of Mount Carmel, originally built as a Carmelite chapel in the 15th century and now the only Carmelite foundation in the British Isles still used for regular worship. Look out too for Plewlands House, built in 1641 and restored recently by the National Trust for Scotland; the 17th-century tolbooth with the Queen Victoria Golden Jubilee Clock, dated 1887; and Hawes Inn, opposite the old ferry pier, which was mentioned in *The Antiquary* by Sir Walter Scott and *Kidnapped* by Robert Louis Stevenson. To get a true picture of the history of South Queensferry it's worth calling into the museum of local history in City Chambers (Tel: 031-331 1851 for details).

South Queensferry is a place to visit at any time of the year, but it really bursts into colour during the second week of August when the annual Ferry Fair is held. The streets are lined with people singing, dancing and making merry! (*See also Kirkliston, page 130.*)

Bus: 43

EXTRA . . . EXTRA . . . The village of Dalmeny is a mile away. Here you can see a fine 12th-century church which was restored in 1937 by the parishioners.

STOCKBRIDGE, 1½ miles (2½km) west of Princes Street

If you've walked down the Royal Mile (*see Walk 3, page 147*) and wandered along Princes Street you'll no doubt be wondering where all the little cafés, restaurants, craft and antique shops are hidden. Well, they're not hidden at all, they're in Stockbridge!

Stockbridge, which is situated on both sides of the Waters of Leith and is only a short bus ride from Princes Street, is one of Edinburgh's most colourful areas. Squeezed between cake shops and chemists all sorts of interesting things are happening. Take a walk down St Stephen Street which is just off north West Circus Place – it's the place to browse among fine antiques and Victorian bric-à-brac. Don't forget to visit the Museum of Lighting (*see page 95*). At the bottom of St Stephen Street is St Stephen Place with its large stone archway. Built in 1824 and designed by Archibald Scott, the archway was the entrance to the meat and fresh produce market which flourished here for over 100 years. There are lots of other interesting pieces of architecture to look out for: 'The Colonies', which were part of a 19th-century co-operative building scheme; Duncan's Land, built during the 17th century, which is the oldest house in Stockbridge and has a plaque above the door which reads 'Fear God Only All Who Enter Here'. It's a good idea to combine a visit to Stockbridge with a quiet walk along the Water of Leith to Dean Village (*see page 127*) or through the nearby Royal Botanic Garden (*see page 26*). Then you'll sample yet another of Edinburgh's startling contrasts of pace – the hectic and commercial alongside the tranquil and peaceful.

Bus: 34, 35

EXTRA . . . EXTRA . . . Many important people have stayed in Stockbridge. They include Sir Henry Raeburn – who gave his name to Raeburn Place – and James Hogg, who worked on *The Queen's Wake* in Deanlaugh Street.

Robert Louis Stevenson (*see Robert Louis Stevenson Heritage Trail, page 58*) was born at 8 Howard Place and Thomas Carlyle lived at 21 Comely Bank when he was first married.

SWANSTON, 5½ miles (9km) south of Edinburgh

Swanston is minute – but perfect! Situated on the lower slopes of the Pentland Hills (*see page 25*) and separated from Edinburgh by farmland, it has preserved its olde-worlde charm. The hamlet is little more than a small cluster of 17th-century thatched cottages, brilliantly white-washed, ringed by tall trees and surrounded by fields. All in all, it's an idyllic spot.

Bus: 4

EXTRA . . . EXTRA . . . Swanston Cottage was described by Stevenson (*see Robert Louis Stevenson Heritage Trail, page 58*) as a 'rambling cathedral'. From 1867 to 1880 his family used the cottage as a summer home.

CHAPTER SEVEN
Walks

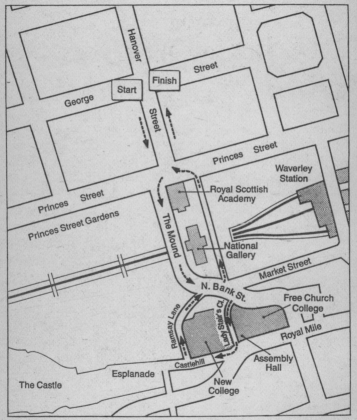

Walk 1 Floodlit Edinburgh

WALK 1 · FLOODLIT EDINBURGH (a walk for after dark)

This is the perfect way to work off a heavy supper. Your walk starts at the statue of King George IV where Hanover Street and George Street cross. The statue, which commemorates the King's visit in 1822, is not itself lit. However, it can be seen clearly as many of the buildings in George Street are brightly floodlit. Look out for the illuminated clock face on the **Church of St Andrew and St George** (*page 39*). From George IV's statue walk down Hanover Street and on to Princes Street. From here you have your first floodlit view of the castle – that's where you'll be ending your walk. It's not as far away as it seems, so keep going! Cross Princes Street and take a look at the subtly lit Academy building. Here begins your long haul up The Mound. On your right is **Princes Street Gardens** (*page 26*) which have unusual lamps near their entrance; on your left is the **National Gallery of Scotland** (*page 96*) lit by wonderful round-headed lamps. Pause and take a good look at **Edinburgh Castle** (*page 42*) from here, it makes quite a spectacular skyline sprawling along the dark mass of its rock. You can see quite a lot of detail and pick out many of the main buildings. Then continue your climb up The Mound. Halfway up it curves to the left and reveals the dramatically floodlit Bank of Scotland. Rest awhile at the junction of Market Street and The Mound, and enjoy the twinkling view of Princes Street, against which looms the sinister silhouette of the

Scott Monument (*page 66*) like a mysterious, nobbly rocket. You will also be able to see the well-lit clock face of the North British Hotel. To continue your walk, turn into **Lady Stair's Close** (*page 48*) – a small alley near a wine bar (the only one in this area). The first building you reach, up a small flight of steps, is **Lady Stair's House** (*page 94*). Lit by a single old lamp, it marks a complete change of atmosphere – you're now in Old Town Edinburgh; a crowded area of towering tenements steeped in history. Entering the second level of Lady Stair's Close is like stepping back in time. This lovely courtyard is worth seeing by day or by night, but after dark and lit by lamplight it's particularly atmospheric. A tiny narrow alley will lead you out on to the top section of the **Royal Mile Walk** (*page 147*). Lights high on buildings make this part of the Royal Mile very bright indeed – and something of a shock after the creeping shadows of Lady Stair's Close. Turn left and walk up the final section of this famous mile. As you walk, look down alleyways and through open doors – you may be surprised at what you see. The Royal Mile narrows and then suddenly there's the castle! Unfortunately you can't enter the esplanade but you can look past the soldiers on duty and enjoy a view of its fortified walls – unimpeded by tourist coaches. This is the end of your walk. Give yourself a pat on the back – you made it! You could, however, do the walk in reverse, but remember to keep looking over your shoulder or you're sure to miss something!

To return to Princes Street, walk down **Ramsay Lane** (*page 57*). Stop to look at Ramsay Gardens – a pretty courtyard illuminated by domestic light which spills from the high tenements. Continue walking down Ramsay Lane – cobbled and steep, it has a dramatic view of The Mound. Cross the road where Ramsay Lane joins The Mound and take Playfair Steps down past the National

Gallery and then walk on down to Princes Street. Here you could do some window shopping or, to complete your route, walk up Hanover Street and back to George IV's statue.

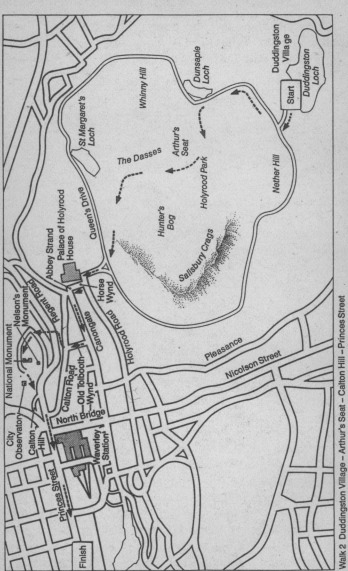

Walk 2 Duddingston Village – Arthur's Seat – Calton Hill – Princes Street

WALK 2 DUDDINGSTON VILLAGE – ARTHUR'S SEAT – CALTON HILL – PRINCES STREET

Starting in **Duddingston** Village (*page 128*), this is a good walk to do in the afternoon – perhaps after a picnic lunch beside Duddingston Loch. From the loch make your way across Windy Goule up towards **Arthur's Seat** (*page 13*), taking a small detour to your right to look at bleak, but duck-filled, Dunsapie Loch. From Dunsapie Loch continue climbing to the summit of Arthur's Seat – it *is* worth the effort. From here you have a fine view of Edinburgh and of **Calton Hill**. When you've got your breath back, and this will take a few minutes, make your way down the north side of Arthur's Seat towards the **Palace of Holyroodhouse** (*page 54*) and the ruins of the Abbey of Holy Rood. When you reach the wrought-iron gates of the palace, stop a few moments and admire its magnificent frontage – some 215 feet (65m) long – and its grand Doric columns. Leaving the palace gates, turn left into Canongate. Part of the **Royal Mile** (*Walk 3, page 147*), there's lots to see here. This walk takes you past the **Scottish Craft Centre** (*page 74*), **Huntly House** (*page 92*) and Moray House on your left, and **Canongate Kirk** (*page 37*) the **Brass Rubbing Centre** (*page 86*) and **Canongate Tolbooth** (*page 87*) on your right. They are all well worth exploring. When you've seen all you want, take the small turning beside the tolbooth, interestingly called Old Tolbooth Wynd, which will bring you to Calton

Road. Next you have a steep footpath up to the **Burns Monument** (*page 36*). The start of this path is not particularly obvious, but you can find it by looking up towards the monument and tracing its route down to the road. The walk up is quite a slog and you'll almost certainly by now have forgotten the windy walk down from Arthur's Seat and be thinking that all Edinburgh's hills are one way – upwards! From Burns Monument cross Regent Road. The building with a massive six columned Doric portico is Royal High School. It was designed by one of its ex-pupils, Thomas Hamilton. Time to walk up again – up Calton Hill (*page 17*). The views from here, in whichever direction you look, are simply fantastic. All Edinburgh, old and new, spreads out before you. The buildings on the hill are the **National Monument** (*page 51*), the Observatory, **Nelson Monument** (*page 52*), and **Dugald Stewart Memorial** (*page 42*). Steps on the west side of Calton Hill will take you down (yes, down at last!) to Waterloo Place. Almost immediately opposite you are **Calton Burying Grounds** (*page 16*) which are worth a look if you've time and energy. If not, turn right and go down Waterloo Place which joins the eastern end of Princes Street – the end of your walk.

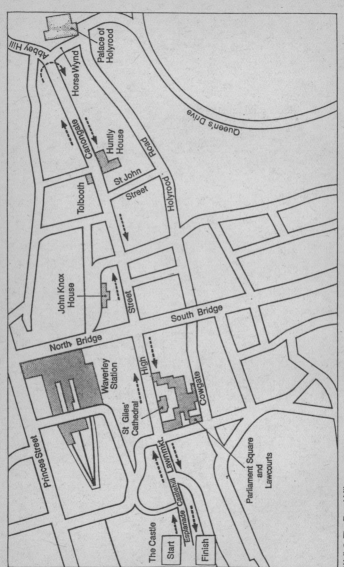

Abbey Hill

Horse Wynd

Palace of Holyrood

Canongate

Huntly House

Queen's Drive

Tolbooth

St John

St John Street

Holyrood Road

John Knox House

Street

South Bridge

North Bridge

Waverley Station

High

Cowgate

St Giles' Cathedral

Lawnmkt.

Parliament Square and Lawcourts

Princes Street

Castlehill

The Castle

Esplanade

Start

Finish

Walk 3 The Royal Mile

WALK 3 ROYAL MILE

Begin on the esplanade of **Edinburgh Castle** (*page 42*). Stop for a while to enjoy the beautiful views then take a deep breath and start the walk – there's an amazing amount of history and interest packed into this mile-long road which stretches from Edinburgh Castle to the Palace of Holyroodhouse. As you leave the castle gates, **Cannonball House** (*page 37*) is on your right. You'll see a cannonball wedged in the gable – supposedly fired back in 1745. Castle Hill leads you into Lawnmarket. Take time to explore all the little closes and read the plaques which tell you about the famous people who have lived and visited here. On your left you'll come to Gladstone's Land, an early 17th-century tenement house, which has been partially taken over by the **Textile Workshop and Gallery** (*Craft, page 75*). The next turning on your left is **Lady Stair's Close** (*page 48*) and the fascinating **Lady Stair's House** (*page 94*), now a museum devoted to three Scottish literary geniuses – Scott, Burns and Stevenson. Lady Stair's House is part of the **Robert Louis Stevenson Heritage Trail** (*page 58*). Opposite is **Riddle's Close** (*page 57*), part of the **Patrick Geddes Heritage Trail** (*page 56*) and **Brodie's Close** (*page 35*), home of the famous Deacon Brodie, the inspiration for Stevenson's *Dr Jekyll and Mr Hyde*.

As Lawnmarket leads into High Street, you can't miss the magnificent **St Giles' Cathedral** (*page 62*) on your right. Look at the ground outside and you'll see the

cobblestones which mark the 'Heart of Midlothian'; tradition has it that it's good luck to spit here! Behind the
cathedral is **Parliament Hall** (*page 55*) and the busy
Lawcourts (*page 77*) An equestrian statue of Charles II
stands in Parliament Square. So too does the **Mercat
Cross** (*page 50*) – the old market cross. A little further
down on your right is **Anchor Close** (*page 35*) and
opposite is **The Museum Shop** (*page 79*) which is the
free-to-enter part of the Edinburgh Wax Museum. You
can see candles being made in the shop. The next point
of interest is Tron Church on your right. Founded in 1637
but now out of use, this is a favourite gathering place to
celebrate **Hogmanay** (*page 119*). Cross the road and you
come to John Knox's House. You have to pay to go
inside but you can still enjoy the olde-worlde feel of this
16th-century timbered house from the outside. There's a
lot of dispute about whether or not John Knox actually
lived here. Next door is the **Netherbow Arts Centre** (*page
99*) which makes an ideal halfway stop if you're feeling in
need of a rest.

Now walk on down into Canongate, poking your nose
into all the little alleyways as you go, until you come to
Canongate Tolbooth (*page 87*) on your left. This is now a
Brass Rubbing Centre (*page 86*) and museum. Opposite
is **Huntly House** (*page 92*) which is well worth a visit. The
displays really bring local history to life. Next door is
Acheson House, home of the **Scottish Craft Centre** (*Craft,
page 74*). On the other side of Canongate stands **Canongate Church** (*page 37*) with its churchyard containing
graves of many famous people. Further on is **White Horse
Close** (*page 68*), a 16th-century royal mews. As you walk
into Abbey Strand with the **Palace of Holyroodhouse**
(*page 54*) directly in front of you, look to your left and
you'll see Queen Mary's Bath, a lovely little house where
Queen Mary was supposed to take baths in white wine!

And now you come to the Palace of Holyroodhouse, official residence of the queen in Scotland. Note the 'S' marks outside the gates, past which debtors could take refuge (*see Holyrood Park, page 21*). There's a charge to go inside the palace so enjoy it from the outside then turn back and walk up to the castle. You'll be surprised at how much you missed on the way down!

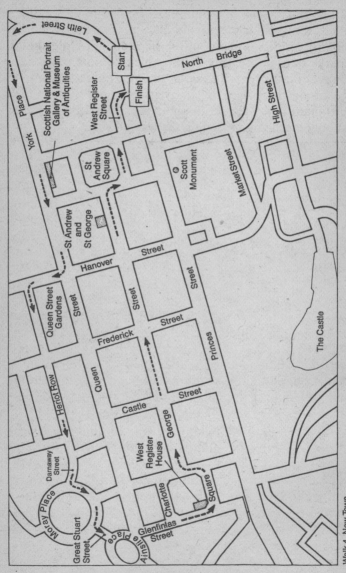

Leith Street

North Bridge

Start

Finish

West Register Street

York Place

Scottish National Portrait Gallery & Museum of Antiquities

St Andrew Square

High Street

Scott Monument

Market Street

St Andrew and St George

Hanover Street

Street

Street

Queen Street Gardens

Street

Frederick Street

Street

The Castle

Heriot Row

Queen Street

Princes Street

Castle Street

George Street

West Register House

Darnaway Street

Moray Place

Charlotte Square

Great Stuart Street

Ainslie Place

Glenfinlas Street

Walk 4 New Town

WALK 4 NEW TOWN

Start your walk outside **HM General Register House** (*page 91*). Stand beside the statue of the Duke of Wellington and look across to North Bridge and the General Post Office, designed by Robert Matheson and built between 1861 and 1866. Inside you'll find the **Philatelic Bureau** (*page 101*). To your right is Princes Street, but turn left and walk up Leith Street. On your left is St James' Centre, a shopping/hotel/office complex built in the late 1960s on the site of St James' Square, part of James Craig's original plan for the New Town in the 18th century. Continue walking with Picardy Place on your right. Conan Doyle, creator of Sherlock Holmes, lived at no. 2. On your right is St Mary's Roman Catholic Cathedral. Turn left into York Place. You come to St Paul's and St George's Episcopal Church (built 1816–18) and then a little further along at no. 36 is the Scottish headquarters of the Pharmaceutical Society of Great Britain. It's well worth popping in to see the **Traditional Pharmacy** (*page 107*). Fully refreshed by the sight and smell of the lotions and potions, continue along York Place, cross over Dublin Street and into Queen Street. On your left is the **Scottish National Portrait Gallery** (*page 104*) which now also houses the **National Museum of Antiquities of Scotland** (*page 98*). To your right are Queen Street Gardens – beautiful to look at, but unfortunately you need to be a key-holder to go in. Turn right down Queen Street Gardens East which leads into

Dundas Street and the **New Town Conservation Centre** (*page 99*). After a visit to the centre, retrace your steps along Dundas Street and turn right into Heriot Row – the height of gracious living! Robert Louis Stevenson lived at no. 17 and opposite is an information plaque, part of the **Robert Louis Stevenson Heritage Trail** (*page 58*). Turn up into Wemyss Place and then left into Darnaway Street and you come to Moray Place where, at no. 28, the Earl of Moray had his town house. Look at the lamps outside the houses as you walk past. With Moray Place on your right, turn down Great Stuart Street and into Ainslie Place. Now turn left into the rather steep Glenfinlas Street and into the celebrated Charlotte Square designed by Robert Adam, completed in 1820 and extremely well-preserved. On the west side of the square you'll see the green dome of what was once St George's Church looming above. This is now **West Register House** (*page 108*). If you're interested in history call in and see their records and exhibition; if you prefer arts, there's an arts information centre just a few doors down at no. 19. Walk along the south side of the square, turn left and then right into George Street. This street was at the centre of the original plan for the New Town and now has lots of interesting galleries, shops and the city's two leading **Auction Houses** (*Auctions, page 71*). Take your time walking along this street. Cross over Hanover Street and on your left is the **Church of St Andrew and St George** (*page 39*). Remember, if you're feeling thirsty, there's a café in the undercroft! At the end of George Street you come to St Andrew Square with its early Georgian town houses on the north side. In the centre of the square stands the statue of Henry Dundas, the 1st Viscount Melville. Look to your right and you'll see the **Scott Monument** (*page 66*). Turn left into the square up the north side, then turn right and a little way along on your left is the **Royal Bank of Scotland** (*page 59*) with the statue of the 4th Earl of Hopetoun at the front. Straight ahead of you is Princes Street – but take a scenic detour down West Register Street, past West Register Place and the Café Royal and you're back at HM General Register House.

Index